STUDY GUIDE FOR

SECOND EDITION

MANAGERIAL ACCOUNTING

Prepared by

SANOA J. HENSLEY
Texas Christian University

GERALDINE DOMINIAK
Texas Christian University

JOSEPH G. LOUDERBACK III
Rensselaer Polytechnic Institute

KENT PUBLISHING COMPANY
BOSTON, MASSACHUSETTS
A Division of WADSWORTH, INC.

Accounting Editor: Jon Thompson

Copy Editor: Carolyn McGovern

Typist: Betty Ritter

Printed in the United States of America

    3 4 5 6 7 8 9 10—82 81 80

CONTENTS

TO THE STUDENT

Designed to complement Louderback and Dominiak's <u>Managerial Accounting</u>, this study guide is neither a replacement for that text nor a substitute for positive and active participation in the classroom. The major emphasis here centers on reinforcing key concepts and providing additional problems for analysis and application of theory. Additionally, problem areas that have troubled past students are considered in the Final Comments section in each chapter.

The guide should be used systematically as the course progresses. Although attempting to work through the guide initially the night before a major examination might gain a few test points, you should use the guide regularly to supplement the text and lectures.

How closely the guide is tied to your in-class activities will, of course, be the decision of your instructor. Answers to the Comprehension Checks and Applications are given in the key; this structure gives you immediate feedback and permits you to use the guide independently.

The format of the first chapter differs slightly from that of the remaining chapters, but beginning with Chapter 2, Profit Planning, the following study sequence is recommended.

1. Guide: Read the Overview and proceed immediately to the section for guided reading, which may be headed Questions for Guided Reading or Statements for Guided Reading. This material follows very closely the exposition in the text and will be of greatest value as a study aid if you read it carefully before you read the text.

2. Text: Read the expository matter in the chapter, stopping immediately after the Summary. Do the Review Problem(s) and compare your results with those provided in the text. Should any parts of your answers differ from those given, try to determine the reasons for the differences.

3. Text: Proceed to the Key Terms and, if applicable, the Key Formulas. See if you can define the Key Terms, checking your answers with the text if necessary. In reviewing the Key Formulas, be sure you understand <u>why</u> the formulas work, as well as <u>how</u> they work and what they are. When you have done this, you should be ready to check your overall comprehension of the chapter.

4. Guide: Work the Comprehension Check section. After you have finished the short-answer test in this section, compare your answers with those in the key at the end of the guide. But do wait until you have completed the test to check your answers. If any of your answers differ from those given in the key, attempt to analyze the reason for the difference. If you need help, refer immediately to the text.

5. Guide: Work the Applications section. Answers for this section are also provided in the key. Carefully review the solutions to any of the applications for which you arrived at different answers.

6. Text: Prepare the Questions for Discussion, Exercises, Problems, and Cases as assigned by your instructor.

7. Guide: Read the Final Comments section, which clarifies material that has troubled students in the past. It should be helpful at this point, to redo any parts of the Comprehension Check or the Applications that you did not do correctly the first time.

INTRODUCTION

OVERVIEW

This chapter explains the functions of management—planning, decision making, controlling, and evaluating—and shows the relationship of managerial accounting to these functions. The chapter also underscores the similarities and differences of financial accounting and managerial accounting and explains five of the major activities of the managerial accountant. As a preview of the initial chapter, read the questions in the following section.

QUESTIONS FOR GUIDED READING

+ What are the two most important functions of management?

+ What does management by objectives entail?

+ What service can the managerial accountant provide when the objectives set by various units within a firm conflict?

+ Of what importance are reports to a manager who employs the principle of management by exception?

+ How do planning and decision making differ?

+ How can performance evaluation influence the actions of a manager?

+ What is the broad difference between a line manager and a staff manager?

+ Other than the managerial accountant, what are some sources that managers use to gain needed information?

+ What is a pro forma statement, and why is a cash budget one of the most important of these statements?

+ In aiding in the decision-making process, why is it important for the managerial accountant to know for whom the report is intended?

+ What is a control report, and what is its use to a manager?

+ How often should a managerial accountant prepare control reports?

+ When evaluating subordinate managers, why does top management rely on the reports prepared by the managerial accountant?

+ Why is the managerial accountant concerned with selecting an appropriate measure of performance?

+ What is the relationship between action and evaluation?

+ What are the raw materials of both financial accounting and managerial accounting?

+ How do the intended audiences for financial accounting reports and managerial accounting reports differ, and how does this influence the content and use of these reports?

+ What classification schemes are used in financial accounting reports?

+ What classification schemes are used in managerial accounting reports?

+ How do the source and nature of information employed in financial accounting differ from those employed in managerial accounting reports?

+ How do Generally Accepted Accounting Principles restrict the managerial accountant?

+ What are five major activities of a managerial accountant?

+ What is a specific example of each of these five activities?

+ What type of professional certification is available for managerial accountants?

Now use these questions as an outline while you read the expository material in the text, stopping at the heading Questions for Discussion. Before you proceed to the Comprehension Check, attempt to define the Key Terms which are listed in the text.

COMPREHENSION CHECK

To help assess your comprehension of this chapter, take the following true-false test. Draw a line through the number of any false statement.

1. Managerial accounting deals with internal information used by economic organizations to determine their courses of actions.

2. The planning function is the process of setting goals and developing methods for achieving them.

3. Management by objectives, an important concept of managerial method, is associated with the performance evaluation function.

4. When an economic organization employs management by objectives, the managerial accountant is often asked to generate relevant information to help resolve conflicting objectives of various units within the organization.

5. In using management by exception, a manager relies on reports to keep informed concerning operations, investigating those operations for which the reports indicate results that deviate from plans.

6. Line managers are subject to the authority of staff managers.

7. Literally, pro forma means "as a matter of form, for the sake of form." Thus, a pro forma statement is one that is made as a matter of form and has little substance or real significance.

8. When preparing reports to aid managers in decision making with regard to a specific product or problem, the managerial accountant should include all available information, thus ensuring that nothing is overlooked.

9. A quantitative analysis prepared by the managerial accountant may not include all the relevant information necessary for a specific decision.

10. A control report details costs that have been incurred and often relates these actual costs to planned costs.

11. Control reports can be used effectively as an aid to management by exception.

12. The selection of an appropriate measure of performance is a problem outside the sphere of responsibility of the managerial accountant.

13. Generally, both the audiences for and uses of financial accounting reports differ from those of managerial accounting reports.

14. The cost classification scheme for a financial accounting report is usually by object of the expense or by function of the expense.

15. The cost classification scheme for a managerial accounting report is usually by behavior of the cost or by necessity for the cost.

16. While financial accounting reports are usually considered general purpose reports, managerial accounting reports are usually designed for specific users and/or to aid in specific decisions.

17. For the sake of uniformity, both managerial accountants and financial accountants should structure their reports to conform to Generally Accepted Accounting Principles.

18. Some major activities of managerial accountants are aiding in information system design, ensuring that the information system performs according to plan, gathering data, undertaking special analyses, and interpreting accounting data.

19. When aiding in information systems design, the managerial accountant should be sure that the output of the system will provide managers with the information they want to see.

20. The managerial accountant should advise other managers concerning the intended purpose and appropriate use of specific managerial accounting reports.

At this point, check your answers with those provided in the key. A brief explanation is given when the statement is false. If you are unable to understand why an answer is true, refer to the discussion in the text.

APPLICATIONS (A BRIEF REVIEW OF FINANCIAL ACCOUNTING)

<u>Problem 1</u>

Given below are a balance sheet at December 31, 1977, and summary transactions or events for the month of January 1978.

A-1 Company
Balance Sheet
December 31, 1977

Current assets:		
Cash	$1,500	
Inventory	3,000	
Total current assets		$ 4,500
Noncurrent assets:		
Office furniture and equipment		8,000
Less accumulated depreciation		2,000
Net noncurrent assets		6,000
Total assets		$10,500
Current liabilities:		
Accounts payable		$ 2,500
Stockholders' equity:		
Common stock, no par, authorized and issued 100 shares	$3,200	
Retained earnings	4,800	8,000
Total liabilities and stockholders' equity		$10,500

Summary transactions or events occurring during the month of January 1978:
- a. Sales of merchandise, all cash, $10,000
- b. Purchases of merchandise on account, $8,000
- c. Payment of accounts payable, $7,500
- d. Payment of rent for the month of January, $400
- e. Payment of wages for January, $1,500
- f. Other miscellaneous expenses incurred and paid during January amounted to $140.
- g. Cost of goods sold for the month was $7,000.
- h. Depreciation of office furniture and equipment was $60 for the month.
- i. Income taxes of 20% of income before taxes were accrued.

Required:

1. Prepare an income statement for January 1978 for A-1 Company.

2. Prepare a balance sheet at January 31, 1978 for A-1 Company.

After you have solved the problem, check your answers with the key.

Problem 2

Given below is a balance sheet for A-2 Corporation at December 31, 1977.

A-2 Corporation
Balance Sheet
December 31, 1977

Current assets:
Cash	$ 4,000	
Accounts receivable	80,000	
Inventory	120,000	
Prepaid items	600	
Total current assets		$204,600

Noncurrent assets:
Land		35,000	
Building	$150,000		
Accumulated depreciation	9,800	140,200	
Equipment	70,000		
Accumulated depreciation	10,000	60,000	
Total noncurrent assets			235,200
Total assets			$439,800

Current liabilities:
Notes payable	$ 50,000	
Accounts payable	70,000	
Property taxes payable	7,800	
Total current liabilities		$127,800

Long-term liabilities:
Bonds payable 8½%, due 2001	100,000	
Total liabilities		$227,800

Stockholders' equity:
Common stock, $2 par value, 100,000 shares authorized, issued and outstanding	200,000	
Retained earnings	12,000	212,000
Total liabilities and stockholders' equity		$439,800

Data for 1978:
a. Sales totaled $450,000, of which $300,000 were on account.
b. Cost of sales for the year was $310,000.
c. Purchases of inventory on account were $280,000.
d. The note payable of $50,000 plus interest of $2,000 was paid.
e. The 1977 property taxes of $7,800 and 1978 property taxes of $8,000 were paid.
f. Wages of $55,000 were incurred and paid during the year.
g. Depreciation on the building is $4,000.
h. Depreciation on the machinery is $5,000.
i. Prepaid office supplies and insurance, $200 and $400, respectively, were "used up" during the year.
j. Interest of $8,500 was incurred and paid on the bonds payable.
k. Collected $320,000 on account
l. Paid $290,000 on account
m. Utility bills of $2,400 were received and paid during the year.
n. Paid $10,000 on 1978 federal income taxes
o. Corporate federal income taxes for the year of 1978 are $12,660.

Required:

1.   Prepare an income statement for the year of 1978.

2.   Prepare a balance sheet at December 31, 1978.

     Check your answers with the key.

    At this point, you should prepare any Questions for Discussion and Problems that your
instructor has assigned from the text.

CHAPTER 2

PROFIT PLANNING

OVERVIEW

This chapter introduces volume-cost-profit analysis, which is commonly used to predict (1) costs that can be expected at different levels of sales, and (2) income. This type of analysis utilizes a behavioral classification scheme which identifies a cost as fixed or variable according to whether the cost is relatively constant or changes as volume changes. Those costs that change in total in direct proportion to changes in volume are classified as variable costs. The difference between the selling price per unit and the variable cost per unit is the contribution margin, the amount that remains to "contribute" to paying for other costs and producing profit. Fixed costs are those that remain the same in total regardless of volume.

Additionally, the chapter explores the uses (and misuses) of average cost per unit as well as the relationship of contribution margin and losses in decision making. The relevant range, the range over which assumed relationships may be expected to hold true, is introduced, and the importance of time as a frame of reference for the relevant range is noted.

In the section on the construction and use of a volume-cost-profit graph, the break-even point is presented. This is the point at which revenues equal costs and at which profits are zero. Target profit determination is explained as a variation of the typical break-even situation, and the use of contribution margin as a percentage rather than as a dollar amount is shown. The chapter concludes with a brief examination of the use of return on sales (the ratio of income to sales) as a measure of results.

QUESTIONS FOR GUIDED READING

In order to preview the chapter, read the following questions before you begin reading, then use them as an outline for your reading.

+ What does the term <u>cost behavior</u> mean?

+ What behavior determines whether or not a cost is classified as variable?

+ Why would a manager be interested in the contribution margin which is forecast for a sales period?

+ What is the relationship between fixed costs and sales volume?

+ What is the relationship between fixed costs and income?

+ What are the major differences in financial accounting income statements and managerial accounting income statements?

+ What must a manager know in order to predict total costs?

+ What is the relationship of the average fixed cost per unit to sales volume?

+ What problem is inherent in the use of the prevailing average total cost per unit to predict total costs for an anticipated increase in sales volume?

+ Why is contribution margin of special interest to the manager of a seasonal business?

+ When a firm forecasts a 75% increase in sales volume, what type of distortion is inherent in predictions based on the prevailing per-unit profit?

+ Within any relevant range, what influence does a change in sales volume have upon the nature of a firm's costs?

+ What factors are assumed to remain constant within any relevant range?

+ Why is there limited reliability in the use of volume-cost-profit analysis when a firm is engaged in long-range planning?

+ What is the break-even point?

+ What information must be available in order to determine the break-even point in terms of the number of units which must be sold?

+ How does the necessary information differ when a firm wishes to project the break-even point in terms of total sales dollars rather than in terms of the number of units which must be sold?

+ In volume-cost-profit analysis, when is target profit treated as a fixed cost?

+ When is it necessary to know the contribution margin percentage rather than the contribution margin per unit?

+ In volume-cost-profit analysis, when is target profit treated as a variable cost?

+ In profit planning, why might it be necessary for a manager to rethink the projected unit sales volume after an initial unit price determination?

+ What danger is inherent when a manager uses return on sales as the sole measure of the firm's profitability?

COMPREHENSION CHECK

Directions: Complete the following multiple-choice questions by placing the letter of the most appropriate answer available in the blank.

_____ 1. Volume-cost-profit analysis is most commonly used to:
    a. determine the accuracy of financial accounting statements.
    b. predict the anticipated worth of the firm.
    c. predict both anticipated costs at differing sales volumes and anticipated incomes.

_____ 2. For volume-cost-profit analysis, costs are classified according to:
   a. function.
   b. behavior.
   c. sales volume.
   d. anticipated profit.

_____ 3. Total variable costs are those that change in:
   a. direct proportion to changes in volume.
   b. inverse proportion to changes in volume.

_____ 4. Contribution margin is the:
   a. percentage of income to sales.
   b. remainder when sales price per unit is deducted from variable cost per unit.
   c. remainder when variable cost per unit is deducted from sales price per unit.
   d. allowance for charitable expenditures in the company's plan for the year.

_____ 5. Fixed costs are those costs that will remain the same in total:
   a. within the relevant volume range.
   b. unless there are changes in volume.
   c. because it is unwise to change them.
   d. despite efforts of management to curtail them.

_____ 6. Income is predicted by:
   a. multiplying variable cost by contribution margin per unit.
   b. deducting variable costs from total contribution margin.
   c. multiplying fixed costs by contribution margin per unit.
   d. deducting fixed costs from total contribution margin.

_____ 7. The total amount by which income will change if sales change is the:
   a. fixed costs per unit multiplied by the increase or decrease in number of units sold.
   b. variable costs per unit multiplied by the increase or decrease in units sold.
   c. contribution margin per unit multiplied by the increase or decrease in number of units sold.

_____ 8. When preparing an income statement for a retail firm using the contribution margin format:
   a. it is necessary to rearrange costs by function.
   b. sales and income figures will be the same as those in an income statement prepared using the financial accounting format.
   c. costs are classified by object.
   d. volume is understated in order to ensure a profit margin.

_____ 9. If you add total fixed costs to the product of variable cost per unit multiplied by the number of units sold you have calculated:
   a. total costs.
   b. contribution margin in total.
   c. cost of goods sold.
   d. gross operating margin.

_____ 10. The average fixed cost per unit is:
   a. constant at any volume level within the relevant range.
   b. dependent upon the variable cost per unit.
   c. dependent upon the level of volume.
   d. independent of the level of volume.

_____ 11. The average total cost per unit is:
   a. an excellent aid in predicting income for an anticipated increase in sales volume.
   b. an excellent aid in predicting income for an anticipated decrease in sales volume.
   c. dependent upon the level of volume.
   d. the same at every level of volume if a company has no variable costs.

_____ 12. In a seasonal business, firms should continue to operate as long as they are generating:
   a. sales.
   b. contribution margin.
   c. variable costs.
   d. fixed costs.

_____ 13. Expressed as per-unit amounts, variable costs:
   a. are constant.
   b. always change with volume.
   c. must decrease as volume changes.
   d. cannot be predicted.

_____ 14. Expressed as per-unit amounts, fixed costs:
   a. are constant.
   b. decrease as volume decreases.
   c. increase as volume increases.
   d. decrease as volume increases.

_____ 15. Return on sales will:
   a. indicate a need for more stringent controls on product quality.
   b. increase as volume decreases.
   c. increase as volume increases.
   d. always remain static.

_____ 16. If a firm has fixed costs, as volume increases the percentage increase in sales will be:
   a. less than the percentage increase in income.
   b. greater than the percentage increase in income.
   c. the same as the percentage increase in income.
   d. based on the historical ratio of income to sales.

_____ 17. The relevant range:
   a. is a stove powered by solar energy.
   b. indicates minimum and maximum limits of volume needed if the assumed relationships can be expected to prevail.
   c. should not be considered when predicting costs and profits.
   d. never affects total variable costs.

_____ 18. Volume-cost-profit analysis is:
   a. not influenced by time.
   b. independent of the operating characteristics of the firm.
   c. exceptionally useful when predicting income for agricultural products.
   d. a relatively short-run device that usually encompasses periods of a year or less.

_____ 19. The break-even point for unit sales is equal to:
   a. contribution margin per unit divided by total fixed costs.
   b. variable costs per unit divided by total fixed costs.
   c. total fixed costs divided by contribution margin per unit.
   d. total fixed costs divided by variable costs per unit.

_____ 20. In a typical volume-cost-profit graph:
   a. the horizontal distance between the revenue line and the total cost line is the amount of profit or loss at any point on the graph.
   b. the vertical distance between the revenue line and the total cost line is the amount of profit or loss at any point on the graph.
   c. the slopes of the revenue and total cost lines should be the same.
   d. the total cost line rises above the revenue line for all volumes greater than the break-even volume.

_____ 21. Which of the following is true?
   a. Management should decide to discontinue operations immediately if volume falls below the break-even point.
   b. Management should decide to discontinue sales immediately if a change in cost structure causes the break-even point to rise.
   c. All other things remaining the same, an increase in sales volume will cause the firm's break-even point to fall.
   d. All other things remaining the same, a decrease in variable cost per unit will cause the firm's break-even point to fall.

_____ 22. When stated in sales dollars, the break-even point is equal to:
   a. variable costs divided by contribution margin percentage.
   b. variable costs divided by fixed costs.
   c. fixed costs divided by contribution margin per unit.
   d. fixed costs divided by contribution margin percentage.

_____ 23. A volume-cost-profit graph should be plotted:
   a. when a firm anticipates unusual increases in volume.
   b. for use only within the limits of the relevant range.
   c. to ensure the accuracy of historical data.
   d. to predict sales and cost relationships for a ten-year plan.

_____ 24. The unit sales necessary to achieve a particular target profit are equal to the:
   a. contribution margin per unit divided by the target profit.
   b. sum of the fixed costs and target profit, divided by the contribution margin per unit.
   c. sum of the variable costs plus the fixed costs, divided by the target profit.
   d. sum of the variable costs plus the target profit, divided by the contribution margin per unit.

_____ 25. When a firm sets its target profit in terms of a specified return on sales, the target profit is treated in volume-cost-profit analysis as:
   a. a fixed cost.
   b. a variable cost.
   c. income.
   d. sales expense.

_____ 26. Return on sales is the ratio of:
   a. fixed costs to sales.
   b. contribution margin to sales.
   c. variable costs to sales.
   d. income to sales.

_____ 27. A firm that insists on a consistently high return on sales:
    a. logically should expect the greatest possible target profit.
    b. will pay the largest dividend to its stockholders.
    c. assumes that variable costs are static.
    d. may have overlooked the influence of volume on income.

Now check your answers with the key. If you fail to understand why an answer you selected is not the most appropriate one, reread the pertinent section of the text before you continue.

APPLICATIONS

Problem 1 Bennie's Belts

Bennie buys belts for $2.50 each and sells them for $6.00 each. He pays a sales commission of 20% of the selling price to the salesperson. Tissue paper, sacks, boxes, and sales slips cost $.30 per belt. Bennie has signed a one-year lease that calls for monthly payments of $300. Last month was Bennie's first month of operation and Bennie's income statement showed:

Sales (120 belts @ $6)	$720
Variable costs (120 @ $4)	480
Contribution margin	240
Fixed costs (lease payment)	300
Loss	$(60)

1. What is the contribution margin per belt? $ _____

2. What is the contribution margin percentage?   _____ %

3. What is Bennie's monthly break-even point in belts?   _____ belts

4. What is Bennie's monthly break-even point in sales dollars? $_____

5. If Bennie sells 240 belts next month, what would his profit be? $ _____

6. Bennie thinks eventually his store can sell 4 belts an hour
    every hour in his 8-hour working day. He plans to be open 25 days
    per month. Therefore, he plans to sell 32 belts a day or 800 belts
    a month. What is Bennie's target or projected profit? $ _____

7. Bennie needs a profit of $800 a month to meet his personal living
    costs. How many belts must Bennie's Belts sell to meet personal
    costs?   _____ belts

8. If Bennie desires a return on sales of 20%, what must sales dollars $ _____
    be?

9. Bennie desires an income per month of $1,200 from the sale of 600
    belts. What must the selling price be per belt? $ _____

Problem 2

Given below are four graphs.

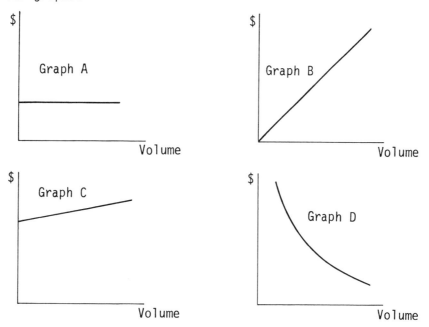

Match the letters of the graphs above to the descriptions below. The graphs may be used more than once.

		Graph
1.	Total revenue line	_____
2.	Total fixed costs	_____
3.	The total cost line	_____
4.	Total variable costs	_____
5.	Sales commissions at 10% of sales dollars	_____
6.	Variable cost per unit	_____
7.	Fixed cost per unit	_____
8.	Revenue per unit sold	_____
9.	A cost that contains both variable and fixed elements	_____

Problem 3

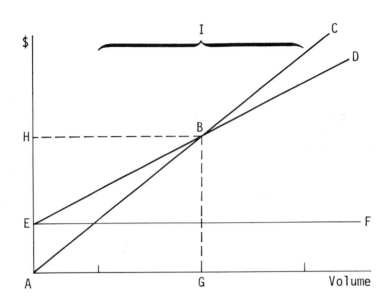

Identify:

AC _____

ED _____

DEF _____

CBD _____

EBA _____

B   _____

G   _____

H   _____

I   _____

EF _____

FINAL COMMENTS

1. The term <u>cost</u> sometimes refers to an asset (an unexpired cost) and sometimes to an expense (an expired cost). In effect, all costs in this chapter are treated as expenses, and your prior experiences in the preparation of financial accounting statements may have interfered with your thinking on this point. Your approach to the term <u>cost</u> should remain flexible. Base your classification of an item as an asset or an expense on the details of each situation.

2. Variable costs per unit remain unchanged as volume fluctuates within any relevant range; total variable costs change directly and proportionately as volume changes.

3. Fixed costs per unit decrease as volume increases and increase as volume decreases; total fixed costs remain unchanged within any relevant range.

4. Variable selling costs are incurred as units are sold. These variable selling costs are expenses and are written off on the income statement. A common mistake of beginning managerial accounting students is to attempt to compute variable selling costs on units purchased or produced instead of limiting this computation to units sold.

5. The break-even point is the point where

   a.   Sales = expenses

      or, to expand the equation,

   b.   Sales = variable costs (VC) + fixed costs (FC)

      or where

   c.   Sales - VC = FC

      or where

                        Total contribution margin = FC

6. $\dfrac{\text{Fixed costs + target profit}}{\text{Contribution margin per unit}}$ = sales in units required for target profit

     and

     $\dfrac{\text{Fixed costs + target profit}}{\text{Contribution margin percentage}}$ = sales in dollars required for target profit

Most students remember the first half of each of these formulas as stated, but they repeatedly forget whether the result of their computation should be stated in units or dollars. It often helps to start with an income statement formula: Sales = variable costs + fixed costs + profit, and to then enter the known items in this formula to solve for the unknown item.

CHAPTER 3

ANALYSIS OF COST BEHAVIOR

OVERVIEW

The previous chapter, Profit Planning, includes an introduction to the behavioral classification of costs as either fixed or variable. Although an either-or approach is valid as an
introduction to this classification scheme, not all costs can be pigeonholed as fixed or
variable. Some of the methods of treating such costs are presented here and how these costs
affect volume-cost-profit analysis is explained. This chapter also investigates measures of
volume other than sales and presents a brief treatment of the relationship of managerial
attitudes to plans for cost structure.

STATEMENTS FOR GUIDED READING

+ Realistic planning for the sales volume necessary to produce a target profit includes consideration of the effect of income taxes on net income.

+ Mixed costs (semivariable costs) include both fixed and variable elements.

+ Mixed costs may be estimated by the high-low method, the scatter-diagram method,·and the
  regression analysis method.

+ The high-low method uses the differences in cost and volume at the extreme points of the
  relevant range, dividing the change in cost by the change in volume to estimate the <u>rate</u>
  of change in cost per unit of volume.

+ The scatter-diagram method charts the total amount of a given cost at various levels of
  volume and uses a line drawn as close to all points as possible to determine the fixed and
  variable portions of the cost.

+ Step-variable costs are present in situations in which a cost changes abruptly at differing
  levels of an operation.

+ The approach used to plan for step-variable costs should be consistent with the underlying
  planning philosophy of the firm, and should be considered by management when actual costs
  and planned costs are compared.

+ Fixed costs can be categorized as discretionary costs or committed costs.

+ Both the long-run effects and the short-run effects of a change in discretionary fixed
  costs should be considered when management initiates a cost reduction program.

+ Although current committed fixed costs cannot be avoided, these costs are subject to review
  when planning for the future.

+ In order to generate accurate planning, the cost under consideration should have a proportional relationship to an appropriate measure of volume.

+ While both the cost of raw material and the cost of direct labor are normally considered variable with the volume of production, manufacturing overhead is a mixed cost which includes fixed and variable components.

+ When planning the cost structure of a firm, one important consideration is the attitude of management with regard to risk and reward.

+ Expressed as either a dollar amount or as a percentage of sales, the margin of safety (MOS) indicates the amount by which sales could decline before the break-even point is reached.

COMPREHENSION CHECK

Directions: Draw a line through the number of any false statement.

1. The sales dollars necessary to achieve a target after-tax profit are equal to the sum of the target profit and the fixed costs divided by the contribution margin percentage.

2. With a rental agreement based on a set fee plus a percentage of sales dollars, rent should be classified as a variable cost since it will probably fluctuate each month.

3. In the high-low method of estimation, the variable portion of the cost is equal to the difference in costs at the extreme points of the relevant range divided by the difference in volume at these same points.

4. In the scatter-diagram method of estimation, the fixed cost component is the point at which the fitted line hits the horizontal axis of the chart.

5. Since regression analysis is a more sophisticated method than either the high-low method or the scatter-diagram method for estimating the fixed and variable components of a mixed cost, the managerial accountant should always employ this method for estimating a mixed cost.

6. For step-variable costs, use of the middle line will produce both favorable and unfavorable variances when actual and planned costs are compared; therefore, the middle line is the least accurate and should be used in planning with extreme caution.

7. Fixed costs may be categorized as discretionary costs, those which can be altered by managerial action, and programmed costs, those which cannot be altered without closing down the business.

8. Since discretionary fixed costs are subject to managerial review and action over relatively short periods, for planning purposes these costs should be treated as volatile.

9. Committed fixed costs are those costs that a firm must incur if it is to continue to exist.

10. Once the managerial accountant identifies what a fixed cost is, the classification of that cost as discretionary or committed is a routine matter.

11. If the committed fixed costs of a firm that is operating at a loss are greater than that loss, the firm should halt operation immediately.

12. Since most costs will increase as sales increase, sales is the most accurate measure of volume available to the managerial accountant.

13. For a manufacturing firm, the cost of direct labor is generally classified as a fixed cost because the firm must have employees who work directly on its product.

14. Expectations concerning future sales levels and fluctuations in future sales, and the attitude of management with regard to risk and reward are important considerations when planning cost structure.

15. The margin of safety (MOS) is the decline in sales that would bring an operation to the break-even point.

APPLICATIONS

Problem 1

Roy desires an after-tax profit of $2,000 per month. The income tax rate is 20% of profits before tax.
   a. What would Roy's monthly profit before taxes have to be in order
      to meet the target profit? $ _____

   b. If fixed costs are $12,000 per month, what must Roy's contri-
      bution margin be per month in order to meet the target profit? $ _____

c. Assume Roy sells boots for $60 a pair. Roy's variable costs are
    $35 per pair of boots sold. How many pairs of boots must Roy
    sell per month in order to reach his target income? $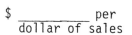

Problem 2

Repairs and maintenance amounted to $2,600 in January and $5,000 in November. Sales in
January and November were $30,000 and $150,000 respectively.

	High	Low
Sales	$150,000	$ 30,000
Repairs and maintenance	5,000	2,600

a. What is the variable component of repairs and maintenance? $  per
                                                                        dollar of sales

b. What is the fixed component of repairs and maintenance? $ _____

c. Write a formula to predict this cost.

    _____

d. Graph the repair and maintenance cost.

e. Sales for next month are estimated at $132,000. Predict the
    cost of repairs and maintenance for next month. $ _____

Problem 3

Given below are two possible income statements for C-3 Company for the next period. Both income statements are within C-3's relevant range.

Sales	$15,000	Sales	$25,000
Variable costs	9,000	Variable costs	15,000
Contribution margin	6,000	Contribution margin	10,000
Fixed costs	5,000	Fixed costs	5,000
Profit before taxes	1,000	Profit before taxes	4,000
Income taxes	300	Income taxes	1,200
Income	$ 700	Income	$ 2,800

C-3 Company estimates sales of $22,000 for the next period. Complete the following income statement.

Sales	$22,000
Variable costs	_____
Contribution margin	
Fixed costs	_____
Profit before taxes	
Income taxes	_____
Income	$ _____

FINAL COMMENTS

1. Students seem to have trouble computing profit before taxes when they know the target profit and the income tax rate. Remember that income taxes are a given percentage of profits before taxes. If you know the target income and the tax percentage, you can always compute profit before taxes in the following manner.

Assume a tax rate of 40% and a target income of $60,000.

Let profit before taxes equal   X
    Income taxes (40%)   .4X
    Income $.6X$ = $60,000

Dividing both sides of the equation by .6,
X or profit before taxes equals $100,000.

2. Sales commissions are a variable cost. Sales commissions are a selling expense and are incurred when units are sold. Sales commissions are not incurred when units are purchased or manufactured.

3. Remember that discretionary costs and committed costs are types of fixed costs.

4. There are three types of manufacturing costs:
    a. Raw material
    b. Direct labor
    c. Manufacturing overhead

A manufacturing cost is a cost that the entity incurs in order to get its product manufactured. Hence, manufacturing costs are also called product costs.

Raw materials and direct labor are variable costs—variable in relation to production. Manufacturing overhead contains both fixed and variable elements. The variable portion of manufacturing overhead varies in relation to production.

CHAPTER 4

ADDITIONAL ASPECTS OF VOLUME-COST-PROFIT ANALYSIS

OVERVIEW

A firm's actual performance frequently differs from its planned performance. As noted in Chapter 3, these differences may indicate the organization's planning philosophy, and they may also be caused by external events, faulty planning, poor management, or situations the firm could neither foresee nor control. Whatever the causes of differences between plans and actual results, managers are evaluated on the basis of the efficiency with which they direct and control their spheres of responsibility.

This chapter details ways to analyze differences between planned and actual income which may be attributed to volume and price fluctuation. Additionally, the chapter shows methods for analysis of the sales mix of multiple-product firms and extends the earlier discussion of the concepts of contribution margin and discretionary fixed costs. Included also is an introduction to volume-cost-profit analysis for not-for-profit entities which generate no revenues and for those which generate both revenues and costs.

STATEMENTS FOR GUIDED READING

+ Based on planned unit selling price, the sales volume variance shows the effect on contribution margin when actual sales volume differs from planned sales volume.

+ Based on actual unit sales, the sales price variance shows the effect on contribution margin when actual selling price differs from planned selling price.

+ Strategies for volume-cost-profit analysis are applicable to multiple-product operations that have a relatively constant sales mix.

+ Complementary products are those that are often sold together, such as canvas and stretchers for oil painting, or products that are used together, such as cassette recorders and blank tapes.

+ Based on a typical sales dollar, the weighted average contribution margin percentage is the sum of the contribution margins of the products of a multiple-product firm expressed as a percentage.

+ Although a multiple-product firm does not experience a constant sales mix, the weighted average contribution margin percentage can be determined from the planned income statement and used in the analysis of actual results.

+ A manager for a multiple-product firm who is considering a change in selling effort to produce an attendant shift in sales mix can determine the overall effect of this projected shift by comparing the weighted average contribution margin percentages of the current sales mix and of the projected sales mix.

+   The horizontal axis of a volume-cost-profit chart for a multiple-product firm shows sales in dollars rather than sales in units.

+   To determine the weighted average contribution margin percentage for a sales mix stated in units, prepare an income statement for a hypothetical batch of these units and then divide the total contribution margin by the total sales dollars.

+   Simulation is a computer-assisted planning technique for which the inputs are various sets of assumptions about such factors as sales mix, selling prices, and sales volumes, and the output includes the predicted levels of profit or loss resulting from the various combinations.

+   A separable fixed cost is one that relates only to a single product or product line; conversely, a joint (common) fixed cost is one that relates to two or more products or product lines.

+   For a multiple-product firm, a discretionary fixed cost may not be avoidable when it is a joint cost.

+   Product margin is the difference between a product's contribution margin and its separable-discretionary fixed costs.

+   When planning, a manager should be aware of the possible interdependence of price and volume and of the varying effects of this interdependence on projected profitability.

+   Although the primary objectives of various economic organizations may differ, any economic organization is concerned with maximizing efficiency, obtaining the best possible results from the available resources.

+   Not-for-profit entities often employ benefit-cost analysis, a counterpart of volume-cost-profit analysis.

+   For deciding whether or not a not-for-profit entity generating no revenues should continue to exist, the key number in an analysis of cost structure is variable cost rather than total cost.

+   In benefit-cost analysis for an organization that generates both costs and revenues, revenues are the potential tangible benefits that result from the existence of that organization.

+   A major problem in benefit-cost analysis for an organization that generates little or no revenues is the selection of an appropriate unit of output to use for the measurement and analysis of results.

+   Given a fixed level of funding, managers of not-for-profit organizations should investigate the alternative ways funds may be spent and the effects these alternatives will produce in relation to the goals of the organization.

COMPREHENSION CHECK

<u>Directions</u>: Indicate the example, definition, explanation, formula, or synonym in Column B which best matches an item in Column A by placing the appropriate capital letter in the blank. Not all of the blanks should be filled in when you complete this comprehension check.

<u>Column A</u>

1. _____ sales volume variance

2. _____ sales price variance

3. _____ sales mix

4. _____ complementary products

5. _____ weighted average contribution margin percentage

6. _____ sales mix stated in units

7. _____ simulation

8. _____ product line

9. _____ separable fixed cost

10. _____ joint fixed cost

11. _____ product margin

12. _____ law of demand

13. _____ not-for-profit entity

14. _____ efficiency

<u>Column B</u>

A. abbreviated form of <u>sales mixup</u>, a situation wherein the sales force disposes of more goods than have been produced, making it necessary for the firm to secure from a competitor merchandise it normally manufactures

B. amount by which the contribution margin differs from the related avoidable fixed costs

C. common cost

D. variable costs minus contribution margin

E. describes an intention rather than results

F. favorable when actual unit sales exceed plan

G. federal legislation invoked to ensure that legal tender can be exchanged for gold reserves on demand

H. fixed cost that relates to a single product or product line

I. Ford's Edsel Division

J. group of similar products

K. knives and forks

L. maximizing benefits from a given level of resources

M. minimum expenditure necessary for a nightclub with an unsavory reputation to remain open

N. pitch used by sales force to describe a firm's product line, often exaggerated

O. planned unit cost times (planned unit sales price minus actual unit cost)

P. postage stamps and glue

Q. price-volume interdependence

R. total contribution margin of all products divided by total sales dollars

S. unexpected activity induced by stimulus over which the firm has no control

T. units sold times (planned price minus actual price)

APPLICATIONS

Problem 1

    Ace Company plans to sell 1,000 units at $15 per unit. Variable costs are $10 per unit. Actual results show that variable costs of $10 per unit were incurred as expected. However, 1,400 units were sold at a price of $14 per unit.

	Planned	Actual
Units	1,000	1,400
Sales	$15,000	$19,600
Variable costs	10,000	14,000
Contribution margin	$ 5,000	$ 5,600

Compute:
    a. the sales volume variance

    b. the sales price variance

Problem 2

    Four-Two Company sells three products. Compute the weighted average contribution margin by two methods.

	Products		
	A	B	C
Planned sales	$1,000	$4,000	$5,000
Variable costs	600	2,400	2,200
	$	$	$

a. Method 1:

    1. Sum the contribution margins of all products. $ _____

    2. Compute total sales dollars. $ _____

    3. Weighted average contribution margin = (1 ÷ 2) = _____ %

b. Method 2:

	Product A	Product B	Product C
1. Compute the contribution margin percentage for products A, B, and C	_____	_____	_____

2. In this problem, total sales are $10,000. What percent of total sales is attributable to products A, B, and C (sales mix)?

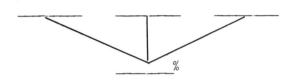

3. Multiply line 1 × line 2.

4. Add the above percentages together to get the weighted average contribution margin.

_____ %

Methods 1 and 2 should give you the same answer.

Problem 3

Omer Company sells 2 packages of hot dogs for every single package of hot dog buns. The cost structures for Omer's two products are as follows:

	Per Package	
	Hot Dogs	Buns
Sales price	$1.20	$.60
Variable costs	.90	.30
Contribution margin	$ .30	$.30

Fixed costs are $5,400 per year.

a. Compute the weighted average contribution margin.   _____ %

b. Compute dollar sales at break-even. $ _____

c. At break-even, how many packages of hot dogs and how many
    packages of hot dog buns are sold?   _____ packages of hot dogs

                                                    _____ packages hot dog buns

d. If profit before tax is $12,000, what are expected sales dollars? $ _____

Problem 4

Below is a current income statement for the Tiger Corporation, which has three divisions.

		Divisions		
	A	B	C	Total
Sales	$40,000	$60,000	$120,000	$220,000
Variable costs	10,000	40,000	80,000	130,000
Contribution margin	30,000	20,000	40,000	90,000
Separable-discretionary costs	5,000	30,000	15,000	50,000
Product margin	$25,000	($10,000)	$ 25,000	40,000
Joint costs				15,000
Income				$ 25,000

Which, if any, of the divisions should be discontinued?

FINAL COMMENTS

1.
$$\text{Sales price variance} = \begin{matrix}\text{actual}\\\text{units}\\\text{sold}\end{matrix} \times \left(\begin{matrix}\text{planned}\\\text{sales}\\\text{price}\end{matrix} - \begin{matrix}\text{actual}\\\text{sales}\\\text{price}\end{matrix}\right)$$

If the actual sales price is greater than the planned sales price, the variance is favorable. Ignoring all the special terminology, selling something at a higher price than you expected to get is favorable.

$$\text{Sales volume variance} = \begin{matrix}\text{planned}\\\text{contribution}\\\text{margin}\\\text{per}\\\text{unit}\end{matrix} \times \left(\begin{matrix}\text{planned}\\\text{sales}\\\text{in}\\\text{units}\end{matrix} - \begin{matrix}\text{actual}\\\text{sales}\\\text{in}\\\text{units}\end{matrix}\right)$$

If the entity sold more units than it had planned to sell, the variance is favorable. Thus, if one of the variance formulas produces a negative result, the variance is favorable.

2.   The weighted average contribution margin is useful when a firm deals with more than one product. Knowledge of the firm's sales mix is needed to compute that percentage. Remember that sales mix is stated as percentages of total sales, either in units or in sales dollars. Even if all products sell at expected prices and the variable costs for each product are incurred exactly as planned, the firm's actual contribution margin may not be as planned because of a difference between planned and actual sales mix.

3.   It should be increasingly obvious that an object classification of costs (rent, depreciation, taxes, advertising, etc.) is of little use in managerial accounting. For the most part, each firm is unique in the manner in which a cost would be classified using the classification schemes that are important for managerial accounting. For example, in earlier chapters you saw that rent may be either variable or fixed or have both variable and fixed components. You also saw that a particular fixed cost might be a discretionary cost in one firm and a committed cost in another. The need to identify costs as joint or separable further emphasizes the need to understand the organization and operations of the individual firm with which you are dealing. As you study the data provided in each new assignment, concentrate on identifying clues as to the classification of costs according to the classification schemes introduced in this book as useful for managerial purposes.

CHAPTER 5

OPERATIONAL BUDGETING

OVERVIEW

This chapter introduces comprehensive budgeting as central to planning, control, decision making, and performance evaluation and explains the reasons for organizing budgets within varying time frames. Comprehensive budgeting includes operational budgets and financial budgets. Operational budgets include the sales forecast, the purchases budget, and the expense budget. Of prime importance to budgeting is the sales forecast, which may be prepared by indicator methods, historical analysis, and judgmental methods, singly or in combination as applicable. When several different sales forecasts are developed by an organization, the expected value concept is a subjective method of arriving at a single forecast figure for use in budgeting. For expense budgets, two methods may be used to develop budget allowances. One method, applicable for fixed costs, sets the budget for a particular cost at a single amount regardless of the volume of activity, and the set figure is termed a static budget allowance. Another method, applicable for variable and mixed costs, sets the budget for a particular cost at a variable amount based on the volume of activity, and the result is termed a flexible budget allowance.

The chapter next introduces some behavioral problems that budgeting sometimes engenders, and then begins an illustration of comprehensive budgeting for the Cross Company, a retailing firm, which illustration is completed in the next chapter. Included here are a sales forecast, a pro forma income statement, and a purchases budget for the Cross Company, as well as an explanation of the purchases budget as it applies to manufacturing firms.

STATEMENTS FOR GUIDED READING

+ A comprehensive budget includes both operational budgets and financial budgets and details the anticipated results for a future period.

+ As an aid to planning, a budget is a formalized system for evaluating means and objectives.

+ As an aid to control, a budget provides an instrument for use in evaluating actual results and for implementing corrective action when necessary.

+ Budgets are usually organized within a specific time frame, the annual budget being the most common.

+ Although it is difficult to forecast in detail for short periods, the annual budget is often broken down into shorter periods in order to measure actual progress in relation to plan and to initiate corrective action if called for.

+ A continuous budget is perpetual with a new time segment added as the current, corresponding segment expires.

+ A project budget is oriented to the completion of a specific task.

+ A capital budget is oriented to the acquisition of fixed assets.

+ The sales forecast is the initial phase of the comprehensive budget.

+ When using indicator methods for sales forecasting, the potential share of the market for an individual firm is projected from the anticipated total sales of the industry.

+ When using historical analysis as a starting point for sales forecasting, it is necessary to consider changes in internal and external conditions which might affect the budget period.

+ Judgmental methods of sales forecasting rely heavily on the "feel" personnel have for the market position of the firm.

+ When a manager employs the concept of expected value, differing sales forecasts are evaluated and assigned probabilities totaling 100% in order to arrive at a single sales forecast for budgeting.

+ In the preparation of expense budgets, a static budget allowance sets the cost at a single amount regardless of the volume of activity, and a flexible budget allowance sets the cost at a variable amount which is dependent upon the volume of activity.

+ Static budget allowances apply to fixed costs, both committed and discretionary.

+ Flexible budget allowances apply to variable and mixed costs.

+ Although the efficiency of individual managers is extremely important, when asked to aid in the resolution of budgetary conflicts of interests, the managerial accountant should consider the efficiency of the total operation more important than the objectives of the individual managers.

+ Although imposed budgets with unachievable performance standards may produce short-range results that appear beneficial, the long-range results tend to be inefficient from the standpoints of both finance and morale.

+ Although imposed budgets may have achievable performance standards, they lack input from those most familiar with the tasks to be accomplished and ignore the important human factor in setting performance goals.

+ Budgets that are used solely as evaluative instruments negate the important function of feedback for corrective action.

+ A budget sets planned limits of cost incurrence; unwise adherence to budgets may result in inefficient expenditures.

+ The purchases budget reflects the inventory level that management deems desirable.

+ Purchases requirements are equal to the total inventory requirements for the time period involved (ending inventory plus expected sales minus the beginning inventory).

+ A manufacturing firm must plan production in terms of units before it can develop a purchases budget in terms of dollars.

+ A production budget details the number of units which must be produced each period in order to satisfy sales and inventory requirements.

COMPREHENSION CHECK

Directions: Complete the following multiple-choice questions by selecting all the appropriate answers and placing the letters preceding these answers in the blank at the right. Sometimes there is no appropriate answer; when this occurs, write NONE in the answer blank.

1. A comprehensive budget for a retailer normally includes:
    a. an income statement for the period.
    b. a balance sheet at the end of the period.
    c. a cash flow statement.
    d. production schedules.
    e. purchasing schedules.
    f. schedules of fixed asset acquisitions.   _____

2. A comprehensive budget:
    a. fosters an intuitive approach to management.
    b. ties together the diverse activities which are related to specific goals.
    c. specifies the means for the achievement of goals.
    d. makes it unnecessary to reconsider initial objectives.
    e. is applicable only to manufacturing firms.   _____

3. A comparison of budgeted and actual results is:
    a. less desirable than a comparison of budgeted and past results when evaluating performance.
    b. a basis for evaluating performance.
    c. rarely done in the "real world."
    d. a basis for corrective action.
    e. an insult to managers who worked to the best of their abilities.   _____

4. Annual budgets are divided into shorter time periods:
    a. as an aid to accuracy, since this tends to eliminate the random factors that influence results.
    b. because this enables top management to pinpoint those managers who are unable to predict weekly sales accurately.
    c. in order to monitor progress and gauge this progress in relation to goals.
    d. in order to institute corrective action when a change in plans appears necessary.
    e. in order to identify varying cash requirements.   _____

5. A continuous budget:
    a. is tied to the completion of a project rather than a time period.
    b. eliminates the need for a separate capital budget.
    c. is a special assignment which is prepared exclusively by the managerial accountant for top management.
    d. has little value for firms with seasonal operations.
    e. is difficult to prepare because almost all firms prepare budgets for the fiscal year.   _____

6. The comprehensive budget begins with the:
    a. sales forecast.
    b. cash flow statement.
    c. pro forma balance sheet.
    d. statement of fixed asset acquisitions.
    e. statement of labor and material needs.   _____

7. Preparation of the pro forma balance sheet and the statement of cash flow presents some technical difficulties because:
   a. they require extension of volume-cost-profit analysis.
   b. it is impossible to control cash flow.
   c. accumulated depreciation may fluctuate.
   d. the leads and lags involved must be recognized.
   e. they exert a negative influence on human behavior. _____

8. As the basis for sales forecasting, the use of an indicator:
   a. requires that the indicator itself is predictable.
   b. is applicable for all firms.
   c. assumes correlation between the sales of the industry and an external economic factor.
   d. is seldom used by firms that deal in consumable goods.
   e. precludes the use of scatter diagrams or regression analysis. _____

9. As the basis for sales forecasting, historical analysis:
   a. provides a starting point.
   b. can be used only when an operation has a record of sustained increases in sales.
   c. can be used only when an operation has a record of sustained decreases in sales.
   d. should be considered in relation to current or anticipated changes in conditions which may affect the sales of the firm.
   e. has been discredited by the National Association of Accountants. _____

10. As the basis for sales forecasting, judgmental methods:
    a. tend to produce conservative forecasts which place the firm in a favorable position at the end of the forecast period.
    b. are based solely on experience.
    c. exclude input from the lower levels of management.
    d. are intuitive in nature.
    e. are less formal than indicator methods or historical analysis. _____

11. The concept of expected value involves:
    a. several different forecasts.
    b. identifying the available alternatives.
    c. assigning probabilities to each alternative.
    d. computing a single forecast figure.
    e. producing end-run goods that the sales force can move quickly because these goods give potential customers more than full value for their dollars. _____

12. Budget allowances:
    a. are the planned cost limits managers can incur in achieving their goals.
    b. represent one of the ways middle management circumvents the income tax system.
    c. negate cost consciousness in a large manufacturing operation.
    d. have seldom been used effectively for control.
    e. are categorized as static or flexible. _____

13. Assuming a framework of consistent cost behavior, favorable variances in a production performance report indicate that:
    a. less has been spent than planned in the budget allowance for budgeted production.
    b. less has been spent than planned in the budget allowance for actual production.

    c. sales have exceeded plan.
    d. actual costs have been less than planned costs.
    e. the firm has experienced a greater volume of production than planned.   _____

14. Behavioral problems related to budgeting can be caused by:
    a. conflict of job interests.
    b. imposition of performance standards that are unachievable.
    c. failure to seek input from those people who actually perform the tasks.
    d. use of the budget as an evaluative instrument without reference to un-
        foreseen changes which occurred during the budget period.
    e. enforcing budget allowances without regard to actual needs to complete
        the task most efficiently.   _____

15. In a purchases budget for a retailing firm:
    a. the inventory level should be equal to two months of budgeted sales.
    b. goods are shown at sales price rather than cost.
    c. goods are shown at cost rather than sales price.
    d. the figures in a row showing the inventory should equal the figure in
        the total column for that row or the inventory account will not
        reconcile.
    e. the ending inventory level is the amount agreed upon by management.   _____

16. A production budget:
    a. is first developed in dollars in order for management to determine the
        number of units that will be available for sale.
    b. contains fixed components.
    c. shows variable costs that fluctuate in proportion to the number of
        units sold.
    d. treats manufacturing overhead as a fixed cost.
    e. treats insurance as a variable cost.   _____

APPLICATIONS

Problem 1

    Four different forecasts of sales were developed by using various market information.
Management assigned probabilities to each of the forecasts. Based on the information given,
calculate expected total sales

Sales Forecast	Probabilities
$600,000	10%
$750,000	50%
$800,000	35%
$920,000	5%

Problem 2

Factory overhead is forecast as follows when production is forecast at 1,000 units.

	Factory Overhead
Indirect labor	$1,500
Supplies	750
Indirect material	500
Repairs	1,200
Depreciation	1,000
Rent	600
Property taxes	300
Insurance	150
Total factory overhead	$6,000

Compute the budgeted amounts for the individual components of factory overhead if production is 1,200 units.

	Factory Overhead
Indirect labor	$_____
Supplies	$_____
Indirect material	$_____
Repairs	$_____
Depreciation	$_____
Rent	$_____
Property taxes	$_____
Insurance	$_____
Total factory overhead	$_____

Write an all-purpose formula for factory overhead cost for this company.

Problem 3

Budgeted production was 1,000 units. Budgeted factory costs were as follows:

	Factory Costs—Budgeted
Material	$2,000
Labor	4,000
Indirect material	500
Indirect labor	1,000
Repairs	700
Depreciation	800
Property taxes	300
	$9,300

Actual production was 1,100 units. Actual factory costs were as detailed below. Revise the above budget for production of 1,100 units. Complete the following performance report. Indicate whether the variances are favorable or unfavorable.

	Revised Budget	Actual Costs	Variances	F or U*
Material	_____	$ 2,310	$_____	_____
Labor	_____	4,290	_____	_____
Indirect material	_____	555	_____	_____
Indirect labor	_____	1,050	_____	_____
Repairs	_____	760	_____	_____
Depreciation	_____	800	_____	_____
Property taxes	_____	300	_____	_____
	_____	$10,065	$_____	_____

*F = favorable; U = unfavorable

Problem 4

Given the following budgeted data for Zero Company for 1980, the first year of operations for this retail store, prepare a forecast income statement for 1980.

Sales price per unit	$12
Budgeted sales in units	4,800
Purchases	5,000 units at $7 each
Sales commissions	$1 per unit
Rent	$300 per month

A fixed salary is expected to be $1,000 per month. All other expenses are expected to be fixed at $150 per month.

FINAL COMMENTS

1.   Because many students who have completed a course in financial accounting have, essentially, memorized the composition of the cost of goods sold section of the income statement, the organization of the purchases budget is not recognized as a simple variation of the formula previously studied. Thus,

> Cost of goods sold = beginning inventory + purchases - ending inventory
>
> CGS = BI + P - EI

is, as the chapter points out, merely a rearrangement of the purchases budget format, or

> Purchases = ending inventory + cost of goods sold - beginning inventory
>
> P = EI + CGS - BI

Prove to yourself that the second formula is equivalent to the first. If you can't remember the basic format of the purchases budget, you can always compute the required purchases by using the more familiar cost-of-goods-sold formula, inserting the known items (beginning and ending inventories, and cost of goods sold) and solving for the unknown (purchases). This can be done in units or dollars.

2.   It is possible to make calculations only if the items involved in the calculation are measured or reported in the same measurement units. You can't add 2 apples and 2 oranges and come to an answer of 4 anything (except maybe "pieces of fruit"). This problem of mixing measurement units arises when working with purchases and sales budgets. Students often forget that the sales budget is measured in sales prices while the purchases budget is measured in purchase (cost) prices.

3.   When making decisions, managers never have all the information they want, nor is it usually possible to obtain information that is exactly correct; they must, instead, operate with the best information available at the time. Flexible budget allowances specifically recognize the need to work with the best available information. Students often try to compare original budgets with actual costs in order to derive variances for performance reports. Remember that the original budget was based on the then available information, namely, budgeted volume (sales, or purchases, or production, or whatever the volume measure being used). When actual amounts (sales or costs) are known, there is also "better" information available about the level of volume; hence, the actual volume is used in computing the flexible "budget" allowance for purposes of comparison with actual costs. This use of actual volume is the advantage of a flexible over a static budget allowance.

CHAPTER 6

FINANCIAL BUDGETING

OVERVIEW

Financial Budgeting continues the presentation of comprehensive budgeting begun in the previous chapter, Operational Budgeting. It details preparation of the cash receipts budget, the cash disbursements budget, and the pro forma balance sheet. Also discussed is the possible need for revising the pro forma income statement as a result of factors brought to light during the budgeting process. Complete budgets are shown for a retailer before moving to the special problems of constructing a cash disbursement budget for a manufacturer.

Having demonstrated the short-term relationships of operational and financial budgets, the chapter next considers annual and long-term budgets, stressing the role of budgeting in asset management and presenting the sources of short-term and long-term financing available. Illustrations of annual and long-range budget preparation extend the application of budgeting procedures, underscoring the necessity for planning the financial requirements of a firm in relation to its anticipated need for assets.

A brief treatment of budgeting for not-for-profit entities reveals the use of expenditures and receipts as the basis for this type of entity, showing the two major weaknesses in traditional budgets of this nature: line-by-line approval procedure and the tendency to base current budget allocations on the prior year's allowance for each line item. Program budgeting and zero-based budgeting are then presented as alternatives to the traditional approach to budgeting for not-for-profit entities.

STATEMENTS FOR GUIDED READING

+ Cash receipts are forecast based on the sales forecast and the firm's previous pattern of cash inflow modified, if necessary, to reflect anticipated changes from those patterns.

+ Cash disbursements for variable costs are forecast based on the purchases budget in relation to the credit terms extended by suppliers, and variable expenses other than cost of sales are forecast in relation to the firm's previous patterns of payment of these costs.

+ When a cash budget is broken down into relatively short time periods, management can anticipate cash flow problems and consider how to deal with these problems before they occur.

+ When the pro forma income statement must be revised, the cash budget must also be revised.

+ The cash budget and pro forma balance sheet are used in planning for asset management.

+ Forecasting cash disbursements for a manufacturer is similar in principle to forecasting cash disbursements for a retailer.

+ The asset side of a pro forma balance sheet is essentially a statement of asset requirements for the budget period.

+ While trade creditors, operations, and short-term loans may be used as sources of some financing, most firms require more permanent financing which is accomplished either through negotiating a long-term loan or by issuing additional common stock.

+ Preparation of an annual budget using percentages of sales during the prior year as a basis for computation of the pro forma income statement assumes that the relationships will remain constant during the budget year.

+ When the initial pro forma balance sheet for an annual budget is completed, the asset side and the equity side will be equal only by chance.

+ If the asset side of the initial pro forma balance sheet is greater than the equity side, management must decide whether the best course of action for the firm is to reduce planned assets or to seek additional financing.

+ The use of the relationships of balance sheet items to income statement items for budgeting is sometimes criticized as oversimplification, especially in the case of fixed assets and accounts payable.

+ In planning for long-term financing for anticipated asset requirements, the choice between debt financing and equity financing is, in some respects, comparable to a choice between fixed costs and variable costs.

+ Although equity financing is less risky for the firm than debt financing, debt financing is used by many firms to attempt to increase the return earned for stockholders.

+ In comparison to budgeting for business organizations, two major differences in budgeting for not-for-profit entities are that the basis for these budgets is usually cash flows and the process often begins with expenditures rather than receipts.

+ Budget authorizations for not-for-profit entities, especially governmental units, tend to be on a line-by-line basis.

+ The two major practical disadvantages of the budgeting process used by most governmental units are the line-by-line approval procedure and the establishment of budgeted line items based on the prior year's allowance for the item, both of which tend to ignore the objectives of the unit.

+ Program budgeting and zero-based budgeting are alternative approaches to traditional budgeting for not-for-profit entities.

+ In program budgeting, emphasis is on desired results, freeing managers to shift expenditures from one category to another in order to increase the probability of the achievement of the unit's objectives.

+ In zero-based budgeting, every proposed expenditure for the budget period must be justified in terms of current conditions and goals and the level of past expenditures is not considered.

COMPREHENSION CHECK

Directions: Draw a line through the number preceding any false statement.

1. Financial budgeting includes consideration of cash flow and financing requirements and the preparation of the cash budget and the pro forma balance sheet.

2. The forecast income statement can be developed using the sales forecasts, and cash receipts for monthly sales should be forecast by spreading payment from customers over a three-month period.

3. A firm whose sales increase steadily and unexpectedly is probably in an extremely favorable cash position.

4. A cash disbursements budget includes payments for purchases, for variable costs, and for fixed costs.

5. When a cash budget is broken down into relatively short time periods, management can foresee anticipated cash deficiencies and alter its plan to alleviate these conditions.

6. When a firm negotiates a short-term loan in order to ensure sufficient cash to meet the requirements of the cash budget, it does so at the risk of adversely affecting sales.

7. Since pro forma income statements and pro forma balance sheets are forecast financial statements, their use is limited to the firm's internal operations.

8. For the purpose of comprehensive budgeting, the production budget for a manufacturer is similar to the purchases budget for a retailer.

9. The planned level of assets usually dictates the planned level of sales.

10. Increases in retained earnings are sources of financing.

11. When a firm has no need to consider sources of financing, its operation is extremely efficient.

12. For long-term financing a firm has two major alternatives, debt and equity.

13. Debt financing is much like a variable cost.

14. Equity financing is less frequently used than debt financing.

15. Not-for-profit entities usually budget on the basis of expenditures and receipts rather than on the basis of revenues and expenses.

16. Budgeting for not-for-profit entities often begins by planning expenditures.

17. The forecasting methods previously studied might be used by nongovernmental not-for-profit entities in the development of a receipts budget.

18. Line-by-line approval procedure tends to increase the efficiency of an operation since this procedure ensures adherence to the budget.

19. Since program budgeting emphasizes results, it is closely related to management by objectives.

20. Zero-based budgeting is an approach to developing the receipts budget.

APPLICATIONS

Problem 1 Budgeting Cash Receipts and Accounts Receivable

Sales forecasts for the first six months of 19X0 follow:

January	$20,000
February	$22,000
March	$25,000
April	$29,000
May	$32,000
June	$37,000

A. If cash sales are 20% of monthly sales, and credit sales are collected 40% in the month after sale and 60% in the second month after sale, how much cash will be collected from customers in April and May of 19X0?

April Receipts		May Receipts	
From April cash sales	$_____	From May cash sales	$_____
From February credit sales	$_____	From March credit sales	$_____
From March credit sales	$_____	From April credit sales	$_____
Total cash from customers	$_____	Total cash from customers	$_____

B. What are the budgeted balances in accounts receivable at May 31, 19X0 and June 30, 19X0?

Accounts Receivable   Accounts Receivable

At May 31, 19X0 = $_____   At June 30, 19X0 = $_____

Computations: Computations:

Problem 2 Comprehensive Problem

Budgeted purchases for the first quarter of 19X0 are given as follows:

January	1,600 units at $5 each,	$8,000
February	1,720 units at $5 each,	$8,600
March	1,880 units at $5 each,	$9,400

Payment for purchases is made the month after purchase.

Other disbursements include a sales commission (paid in the month incurred) of $1 per unit and fixed expenses of $2,500 per month. The fixed expenses mentioned above do not include a depreciation charge of $600 per month. Income taxes (at 40%) are paid in January, April, July, and October for the preceding quarter.

The selling price per unit is $10. Sales in units are projected at 1,500 for January, 1,600 for February, and 1,720 for March. Sales are collected 50% in the month of sale and 50% in the month after sale.

Below is a pro forma balance sheet at January 31, 19X0.

Budgeted Balance Sheet
January 31, 19X0

Assets		Equities	
Cash	$ 3,600	Taxes payable	$ 1,160
Accounts receivable	7,500	Accounts payable	8,000
Inventory	9,000	Common stock ($10 par)	40,000
Furniture and equipment	50,400	Retained earnings	3,340
Accumulated depreciation	(18,000)		
	$52,500		$52,500

A.   Prepare a budgeted schedule of cash disbursements for the month of February 19X0 and for the month of March 19X0.

February 19X0:   March 19X0:

_____   _____

_____   _____

_____   _____

_____   _____

_____   _____

B.   Complete the following budgeted income statement for February 19X0:

Sales	$_____
Cost of sales	_____
Gross profit	_____
Variable selling expenses	_____
Contribution margin	_____
Fixed costs	_____
Income before taxes	_____
Tax	_____
Net income	_____

C.   Complete the following budgeted balance sheet at February 28, 19X0:

Assets		Equities	
Cash	$_____	Accounts payable	$_____
Accounts receivable	_____	Taxes payable	_____
Inventory	_____		
Furniture and equipment	_____	Common stock	_____
Accumulated depreciation	_____	Retained earnings	_____
	$_____		$_____

Computations:

FINAL COMMENTS

When confronted with the sales and purchases budgets (in Chapter 5), and then the cash budgets and pro forma balance sheet (in Chapter 6), students often try to memorize the formats for the various budgets as though these items were completely separate from anything they had studied before. Yet budgets, including pro forma financial statements, are only slight variations of the basic recording procedures learned in financial accounting. In financial accounting one learns to make journal entries for such basic business transactions as sales, purchases, collections and payments on account, and disbursements for or accruals of revenues and expenses. The only difference between budgeting (a managerial accounting task) and recording (a financial accounting task) is that the numbers for the "journal entries" are estimates rather than actual amounts. Hence, if you feel more comfortable with journal entries and T-accounts, think of the budgeting process as a simple matter of making entries or analyzing accounts. A cash budget is no more than an educated guess about the debits and credits that will be in a Cash account. Pro forma statements are no more than normal financial statements resulting from ordinary journal entries posted to typical ledger accounts. When you have trouble coming up with some amount that must be shown in a pro forma statement or a cash budget, try to visualize the journal entries and T-accounts appropriate to that particular item.

SHORT-TERM DECISION MAKING

OVERVIEW

Chapter 7 explains the analytical procedures used to determine the best use of a firm's existing resources in the short run. Although qualitative factors may influence the final decision, analysis of decision alternatives begins with quantifiable factors; the basic consideration is the determination of which choice will produce the highest net income for the firm. This type of analysis is concerned with future revenues and costs, classified as differential (incremental). Revenues and costs already realized or incurred are relevant only as they may aid in predicting future revenues and expenses. Thus, amounts paid for assets in the past, classified as sunk costs, are irrelevant in this type of analysis. Conversely, opportunity costs, the costs of a benefit foregone as the result of selecting a different alternative, are relevant.

The chapter continues with an explanation of segment analysis, details of the areas into which an organization's activities may be divided for analysis. Important here are the profitability of individual segments and the realization that joint costs, regardless of how allocated, remain unavoidable and will not disappear if an individual segment is dropped.

From the discussion of allocated costs, the chapter moves to typical short-range decision-making situations: dropping a segment, complementary effects and the use of loss leaders, make-or-buy decisions, joint products and split-off sales, special orders, and the use of fixed facilities. Important throughout is the recognition that these decisions pertain to the future, that the quantifiable factors to be considered are differential (incremental) revenues and costs and opportunity costs.

The chapter concludes with a brief introduction to legal constraints on decision making, giving specific attention to the Robinson-Patman Act which forbids discriminatory pricing and is enforced by the Federal Trade Commission.

QUESTIONS FOR GUIDED READING

+ In what time frame can short-term decision making be placed, and with what is this type of decision making usually concerned?

+ What is the starting point in considering possible decision alternatives, and what is the basic rule to consider at this level of analysis?

+ What time period is the concern of differential (incremental) revenues and costs?

+ Of what relevance are revenues and costs that have already been realized or incurred?

+ How important are sunk costs in relation to short-term decision making?

+ What types of costs related to existing assets are important, and why is this so?

+ What costs are critical in segment analysis?

+ What reasons are given for including allocated costs in segment reports?

+ What is an incremental loss?

+ What is the relationship of opportunity cost to incremental profit?

+ What are complementary effects, and how do they affect decision making?

+ What are some of the qualitative factors that should be considered in a make-or-buy decision?

+ What is the split-off point, and how do the costs incurred prior to split-off influence decision making?

+ Why is planned production important when considering whether to sell at split-off or to continue processing a product that incurs additional fixed costs?

+ What is the relationship between incremental profit from operating a joint process and the unavoidable fixed costs of operating that process?

+ In special-order decisions, what costs should be considered?

+ What are some of the nonquantifiable factors that affect special-order decisions?

+ With regard to the use of fixed facilities, when might a firm decide to produce a product that is less profitable than another to produce?

+ What are some environmental constraints that influence decision making?

+ What is the purpose of the Robinson-Patman Act, and how does this Act influence short-term decision making?

COMPREHENSION CHECK

Directions: Complete the following statements with the appropriate word(s).

1. In a purely quantitative analysis, the consideration of alternatives should result in

    the selection of the alternative that promises the highest _____ _____

    _____ _____ _____.

2. _____ _____ revenues and costs are the only revenues and costs that matter in decision making.

3. Amounts paid for assets in the past are _____ _____.

4. A benefit that is foregone when an alternative course of action is chosen is termed

    an _____ _____.

5. The major quantifiable factors in short-term decision making are _____ revenues and costs and _____ costs.

6. The areas of activity into which a firm may be divided for analysis are its _____.

7. Joint costs identified in segment analysis are _____ and should not be considered incremental.

8. Allocated costs are _____ costs.

9. The reduction in net income which would occur if a firm decided to drop a segment is called an _____ _____.

10. The choice between an available opportunity cost and the current incremental profit should be based on which is the _____ of the two.

11. Since the decision to continue or drop a segment should be based on total profits, management may need to consider _____ effects in order to make the decision.

12. A loss leader might be expected to show a _____ contribution margin.

13. In a make-or-buy decision, if the purchase price plus the unavoidable fixed overhead is less than the total cost to make a component part, the firm should _____ the part.

14. A manufacturing process that invariably produces two or more separate products is called a _____ _____.

15. The _____ point is the point at which separate products emerge from a joint process.

16. In analyzing whether to see a product at split-off or to process it further, all costs prior to split-off are considered _____ costs.

17. In a special-order decision, the only quantifiable elements relevant to the decision are the _____ ones.

18. Decisions involving the use of _____ _____ are concerned with capacity limitations when two or more products could be sold in various combinations.

19. The Robinson-Patman Act forbids _____ _____.

APPLICATIONS

Problem 1 Segment Analysis

DFW has 3 divisions. A current income statement is as follows.

	Division			
	D	F	W	Total
Sales	$108,000	$109,600	$200,000	$417,600
Variable costs	65,000	54,000	80,000	199,000
Contribution margin	43,000	55,600	120,000	218,600
Fixed costs:				
Division manager's salary	(20,000)	(25,000)	(30,000)	(75,000)
Joint costs—committed, divided equally among the divisions	(30,000)	(30,000)	(30,000)	(90,000)
Income	($ 7,000)	$ 600	$ 60,000	$ 53,600

A. Should D be dropped?

B. How much will total income be affected if D is dropped?

C. Prepare an income statement without Division D.

Problem 2 Make or Buy

Zebra Corporation is currently manufacturing Z part and incurring the following costs:

Material	$20,000
Labor	5,000
Variable overhead	3,000
Fixed overhead	4,000
Total cost to manufacture	$32,000

Z part can be purchased from an outside supplier for $30,000 cash. Should Zebra buy Z part? (Zebra does not have an alternative use for its fixed facility that gives rise to the fixed overhead.)

Problem 3 Special Order

Hi-ups, a shoe manufacturer, has a factory with an annual plant capacity of 20,000 pairs of shoes. Recently, production and sales have averaged about 16,000 pairs annually. The current revenue and cost structure is as follows:

Selling price per pair	$30
Variable manufacturing costs per pair	$12
Fixed manufacturing cost (annually)	$40,000
Variable sales commissions	$3 per pair
Fixed general and administrative costs (annually)	$60,000

Recent internal reports show that the profit per pair of shoes is $8.75, computed as follows:

Sales		$30.00
Variable manufacturing	$12.00	
Variable selling	3.00	15.00
Contribution margin		$15.00
Fixed manufacturing	2.50	
Fixed general and administrative	3.75	6.25
Income		$ 8.75

Low-downs has offered to buy 3,000 pairs of shoes at $20 per pair. The president of Hi-ups has rejected the offer because the $20 selling price is below the cost of $21.25 per pair ($15.00 + $6.25).

If current sales of 16,000 pairs of shoes at $30 each would not be affected by the special order by Low-downs, how much profit did the president reject?

Problem 4 Limited Facilities

Limited, Inc. has a maximum plant capacity of 600 labor hours per week. Fifteen men working 40 hours per week constitutes full capacity. The men and machinery can produce products T and G.

T's Cost Structure		G's Cost Structure	
Material 1 lb. @ $4	$ 4.00	Material 1/2 lb. @ $3	$1.50
Labor 2 hrs. @ $8	16.00	Labor 1/2 hr. @ $8	4.00
Variable overhead 2 hrs. @ $1	2.00	Variable overhead 1/2 hr. @ $1	.50
Fixed overhead 2 hrs. @ $1	2.00	Fixed overhead 1/2 hr. @ $1	.50
Cost to manufacture	$24.00	Cost to manufacture	$6.50
Variable cost to sell	$ 3.00	Variable cost to sell	$1.00
	$27.00		$7.50

Product T sells for $30 per unit. Product G sells for $10 per unit. Demand is such that any units produced can be sold at the above prices. Fixed selling and administrative expenses are $26,000 annually.

A.   What is the contribution margin of a T? $_____

B.   What is the contribution margin per hour if T's are produced? $_____

C.   What is the contribution margin of a G? $_____

D.   What is the contribution margin per hour if G's are produced? $_____

E.   What are total fixed costs per week? $_____
                                                                          per week

F.   Prepare a weekly income statement as if only T's were produced. Use the contribution margin format as below.

Sales $_____
Variable costs:
   Manufacturing $_____

   Selling $_____ $_____

Contribution margin $_____
Fixed costs:
   Manufacturing $_____

   Selling and administrative $_____ $_____

      Income per week $_____

G.   Prepare a weekly income statement as if only G's were produced. Use the contribution margin format:

Sales $_____
Variable costs:
   Manufacturing $_____

   Selling $_____

Contribution margin $_____
Fixed costs:
   Manufacturing $_____

   Selling and administrative $_____

      Income per week $_____

H.   Which of the products should be produced?

Problem 5   Joint Costs and Joint Products

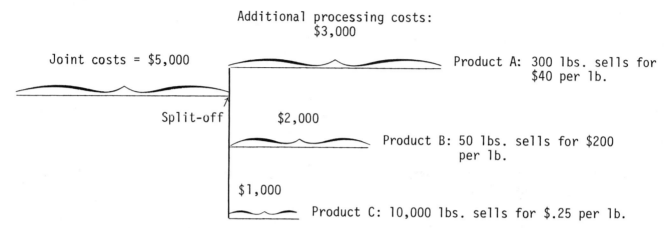

A has a sales value of $6,000 at split-off.
B has a sales value of $9,000 at split-off.
C has no sales value at split-off.

A.   Which products should be sold at split-off?

B.   Assume that the joint costs are allocated $2,000 to product A and $3,000 to product B and that the firm sells only B at split-off. Prepare a product line income statement.

	Product A	Product B	Product C	Total
Sales				
Costs:				
Joint costs				
Additional processing costs				
Income				

FINAL COMMENTS

By this time, you have been introduced to more than a dozen modifiers for the term cost, and it would be worthwhile to find the distinctions and relationships among them.

First, there are the modifiers explaining basic cost behavior: variable, semivariable, mixed, and fixed. Then, there are the modifiers that describe types of fixed costs: discretionary and committed. Next, you learned of modifiers that identified costs in relation to segments of an entity (joint and separable) and to decisions about the existence of those segments (avoidable and unavoidable).

In this chapter you encountered a concept closely allied to the idea of avoidability, namely, the incremental cost. This term refers to costs to be incurred depending on a given decision. Finally, you saw sunk costs and opportunity costs. The former relates to costs incurred in the past; the latter relates to costs not incurred at all, in the normal sense of the word incurred, but rather to a sacrifice made.

You should understand that all costs—past, present, or future—must exhibit some type of behavior and are therefore either variable, semivariable, mixed, or fixed.

CHAPTER 8

LONG-TERM DECISION MAKING CAPITAL BUDGETING, Part I

OVERVIEW

Usually involving additional investments of cash in long-lived assets and returns over an extended time period, capital budgeting decisions should be predicated on the best uses of available capital. Important here is a comparison of the anticipated rate of returns in relation to the cost of capital rather than the comparison of incremental revenues in relation to incremental costs, which is important in short-term decision making.

Although capital budgeting situations may involve investments to reduce costs, this chapter concentrates on investments to increase revenues. Four types of capital budgeting techniques are presented: the net present value method, the time-adjusted rate-of-return method, the payback period method, and the book-rate-of-return method. The first two, the net present value method and the time-adjusted rate-of-return method, may be categorized as discounted cash flow techniques, and because they recognize the time value of money, these discounted cash flow techniques are conceptually superior to the payback period method and the book-rate-of-return method.

An awareness of the effect of the acquisition of depreciable assets on cash flows in relation to taxes is important to understanding the choices entailed in capital budgeting.

STATEMENTS FOR GUIDED READING

+ For capital budget decisions, the expected rate of return on the capital investment should be greater than the cost of capital.

+ Cost of capital is the percentage cost of obtaining the capital resources for a firm's operations.

+ When creditors are the source, the cost of capital is the effective interest rate.

+ When owners are the source, the cost of capital is based on the expectations of investors; simply stated, this is expected earnings per share divided by expected future market price of the share.

+ The cost of capital is the cut-off rate of return, the minimum rate of return that should be acceptable for an investment in a new project.

+ The target rate of return is a specified minimum acceptable rate of return that a firm adopts instead of using cost of capital.

+ Capital budgeting decisions usually involve decisions to increase revenues or to reduce costs.

+ Consideration of the time value of money is essential to investment decisions that involve returns for more than one year.

+ Two of the techniques used to supply information for capital budgeting decisions are:

  1. to compute the time-adjusted rate of return and compare it to the cost of capital.
  2. to use the cost of capital to find the present value of future cash flows and compare it with the cost of the investment.

+ Broadly, for short-term decisions, the change in future income is equivalent to the change in cash flow; for long-term decisions involving the acquisition of depreciable assets, changes in future income are affected by the acquisition of the asset but are not equivalent to the change in cash flow since depreciation expense reduces income without reducing cash flows.

+ All management decisions that involve the future are estimates rather than certainties.

+ When using the net present value (excess present value) method, if the present value of future cash flows is greater than the required investment, the investment is desirable.

+ For investment decisions, the net cash flow is the important factor rather than whether the flow is caused by increased revenues or reduced cash costs.

+ The reduction in taxes resulting from depreciation on assets is called the tax shield from depreciation.

+ Although the present value of an investment will differ depending on the method of depreciation used, the total cash flows from that investment will remain the same as long as there is no change in the tax rate.

+ Since an accelerated depreciation method increases the present value of future cash flows, most firms employ one of these methods for tax purposes; for planning, managers should be aware that straight-line depreciation may be advantageous if the tax rate is expected to increase.

+ The cash flow from the salvage value of an asset should be isolated and discounted separately in an analysis of the present value of an investment.

+ For the quantifiable aspects of decisions, when the net present value method is used for analysis, a project with a positive net present value should be accepted; when the time-adjusted rate-of-return method is used, a project with a rate of return greater than the cost of capital should be accepted.

+ The payback method of analysis evaluates the rapidity with which an investment will be recovered regardless of the anticipated life of the project.

+ The payback method emphasizes return _of_ investment but ignores return _on_ investment and fails to consider the timing of anticipated cash flows.

+ The book-rate-of-return method of analysis is the annual book income divided by the average book investment.

+ The book-rate-of-return method misstates the true rate of return when cash flows and net income are uniform and fails to consider the timing of anticipated cash flows.

+ The net present value method and the time-adjusted rate-of-return method are called discounted cash flow techniques; the important difference between these methods and the payback and book-rate-of-return methods is that the former recognize the time value of money.

COMPREHENSION CHECK

<u>Directions</u>: Indicate the example, definition, explanation, formula, or synonym in Column B that best matches an item in Column A. Not all blanks should be filled in when you complete this comprehension check.

<u>Column A</u>

_____ 1. capital budgeting decisions based on quantifiable factors

_____ 2. cost of capital

_____ 3. tax shield

_____ 4. cut-off rate of return

_____ 5. accelerated depreciation

_____ 6. book-rate-of-return technique

_____ 7. target rate of return

_____ 8. net present value method

_____ 9. salvage value

_____ 10. time-adjusted rate-of-return method

_____ 11. discounted cash flow technique

_____ 12. loss on disposal of plant asset

_____ 13. payback period technique

<u>Column B</u>

A. desirable if incremental costs are less than incremental revenues

B. desirable if the cost of capital is less than the expected rate of return.

C. percentage cost to obtain capital resources for a firm's operation

D. point at which a not-for-profit entity such as a school or welfare agency no longer expects its clients to return

E. minimum acceptable rate of return, often adopted by firm without any real analysis

F. economic theory which emphasizes the necessity to spend dollars quickly during periods of escalating inflation

G. excess present value method

H. project's rate of return compared with cost of capital

I. income tax reduction obtained through asset depreciation

J. net proceeds from sale of remainder of product line not accepted by consumers

K. increases the present value of future cash flows

L. evaluates rapidity of recovery of investment; ignores profitability

M. fails to consider timing of cash flows; misstates true rate of return when cash flows and net income are uniform

N. considers the timing of expected cash flows.

O. account title in annual reports that might indicate poor capital budgeting decisions

APPLICATIONS

Problem 1

E-Z just paid $120,000 for a new machine. The machine has a zero salvage value and a life of three years. The machine will generate additional annual cash revenues of $72,000. The company plans to use straight-line depreciation and expects a tax rate of 25%.

A.   Determine net cash flow for each of the three years.

Tax Computation		Cash Flow
Revenue	$_____	$_____
Depreciation	$_____	
Taxable income	$_____	
Tax	$_____	_____
Annual net cash flow		$_____

B.   Compute the payback periods.

$_____ divided by $_____ equals _____ years.

C.   If the minimum desired rate of return is 24%, what is the net present value of the machine?

Present value of future net cash flows:

$_____ times 1.981 = $_____

Cost of machine $_____

Net present value $_____

D.   What is the average book rate of return of the machine?

1.   Average annual net income $_____

2.   Average book value of the machine $_____

3.   Average book rate of return   _____% (1 divided by 2)

E. If the annual net cash flows were to drop to $60,000 per year, would the investment be earning the 24% desired rate of return?

Problem 2

Cost of special purpose machine	$34,000
Expected useful life	10 years
Expected residual value at end of useful life	$2,000
Tax rate	25%
Depreciation	straight-line
Annual savings in cash operating costs	$9,600

A. Compute net cash flow for year two by completing the following schedule:

Annual savings in cash operating costs $_____

Less depreciation $_____

Income before taxes $_____

Taxes (25%) $_____

Net income $_____

Add back depreciation $_____

Net cash flow $_____

B. Compute payback period.   _____ years

C.   The cutoff rate of return is 20%.

Use the following factors to compute present value of future net cash flows and the net present value of the machine.

Present value of $1, when N = 10 and I = 20% is .162.
Present value of annuity of $1, when N = 10 and I = 20% is 4.192.

   Present value of future net cash flows $_____

   Net present value $_____

D.   Should the machine be purchased?

E.   Estimate the internal rate of return.   _____%

Problem 3

Turkey, Inc. just paid $160,000 for a new machine. The machine has a 3-year useful life and a salvage value at the end of the third year of $50,000. The machine will generate additional cash revenues over additional cash operating costs of the following:

	Net
For the first year	$96,000
For the second year	$54,000
For the third year	$37,000

Turkey, Inc. believes in rapid write-off of depreciable assets and will use sum-of-the-years'-digits. Assume a 50% tax rate.

A.   Complete the following schedule to arrive at net cash flow for years 1, 2, and 3.

	Year 1	Year 2	Year 3
Cash revenues less cash operating costs	$_____	$_____	$_____
Less depreciation	$_____	$_____	$_____
Income before taxes	_____	_____	_____
Taxes (50%)	_____	_____	_____
Net income	_____	_____	_____
Add back depreciation	_____	_____	_____
Cash provided from sale of machine			_____
Net cash flow	_____	_____	_____

B.   The minimum desired rate of return is 10%.

Use the following factors to determine the net present value of machine.

Present value of $1 when N = 1 and I = 10% is .909.
Present value of $1 when N = 2 and I = 10% is .826.
Present value of $1 when N = 3 and I = 10% is .751.

Present value of net cash flow at end of year 1 $_____

Present value of net cash flow at end of year 2 $_____

Present value of net cash flow at end of year 3 $_____

   Total   _____

  Cost of machine $_____

  Net present value $_____

C.   Did the company make the correct decision when it purchased the machine?

D.   What is the payback period?   _____ years

Problem 4

Heights Drive-in Restaurant currently buys its hot dog buns at $.12 per bun and uses 200,000 buns per year. If Heights purchases a special hot dog bun oven for $8,000 and makes the buns expected to be used, the machine could produce a bun for a variable cost of $.08. The $.08 per bun would include material, labor, and variable overhead but would not include the cost of the new machine. The only other cost associated with making the buns would be the fixed cash operating cost of $1,500 annually.

The oven should last for slightly more than four years and would have no salvage value. The firm's cost of capital is 10% and its tax rate is 40%.

Should the oven be acquired?

FINAL COMMENTS

1.   The errors made most often by students studying capital budgeting for the first time involve failure to carefully distinguish between cash flows and amounts on the income statement, tax return, or other accounting reports. Students will, for example, erroneously treat depreciation as a cash flow, compute income taxes without regard to depreciation, or simply ignore the tax outflow associated with income taxes. To avoid such errors, be sure to use two columns in each analysis, one for cash flows and one for the tax computation. And remember that the depreciation in which you are interested is the amount that will show on the tax return, not the amount that will show on the income statement.

2.   Remember that there is a relationship between the answers you develop under the net present value and the internal-rate-of-return approaches. If the cost of capital is used as the discount rate under the net present value approach, a project with a positive net present value also has an internal rate of return greater than the cost of capital. Similarly, if some type of minimum rate is used as the discount rate, a project with a positive net present value also has an internal rate of return greater than the minimum rate required. You can use this known relationship to check the reasonableness of your answer to a problem that uses one or both methods.

CHAPTER 9

CAPITAL BUDGETING, Part II

OVERVIEW

This chapter continues the exposition of capital budgeting techniques, focusing on some specific types of capital budgeting decisions that extend the framework established in Chapter 8. Three special cases considered are decisions requiring an additional investment in working capital, those involving replacing an already existing asset, and those involving disinvestment.

Many investment proposals require an increase in working capital elements such as accounts receivable and inventory in addition to an increase in noncurrent assets such as plant and equipment, and the minimum desired rate of return must be earned on both current and noncurrent assets. Replacement decisions typically involve a firm's essential operations and focus on how these operations are to be performed. Two methods available for evaluating replacement decisions are the incremental approach and the total project approach. Both of these approaches should give the same results.

Analysis for disinvestment decisions is much the same as for acquisition decisions but the point of view is shifted: the firm must compare the savings derived from the asset's use with the opportunity cost of using it. The necessity for this type of decision occurs when the market life of a product is not expected to extend past the life of the asset.

Mutually exclusive alternatives exist when two or more solutions to a problem exist and the selection of one solution precludes choosing any other solutions. In the choice of mutually exclusive alternatives, an analysis must make the choices comparable; for instance, the useful life of one alternative may differ from the useful life of another. For ranking investment opportunities, some accountants use the profitability index rather than the net present value method or the internal-rate-of-return method. It should be noted, however, that the only time a project with a higher profitability index or a higher internal rate of return should be chosen in preference to a project with a higher net present value is when choice of the former will enable the firm to invest additional cash at a rate greater than the cost of capital and this investment opportunity is unavailable if the higher net present value project is chosen.

Previous analyses have been concerned with the determination of whether or not a project could be expected to earn at an acceptable rate based on estimates of its useful life and expected cash flows for the project. Sensitivity analysis approaches evaluation from a different direction, trying to determine what cash flow or what useful life would be necessary if a project is to produce the desired rate of return.

Prior chapters have treated income taxes as if a single rate applied to all the revenues and expenses of a firm. This assumption is invalid, however, since progressive tax rates exist and apply to certain taxpayers, and capital gains are taxed at special rates. Income taxes have also been treated as though they were affected only by revenues and expenses. This assumption is also invalid, since the government provides for carryback and carryforward of operating losses and also permits a tax reduction, the investment tax credit, to entities based on the acquisition cost and life of certain types of assets.

Externalities are social costs or social benefits. These costs and benefits do not affect the operation of an entity directly. Social costs and social benefits are critical in decisions made by governmental units. Problems of measurement, determination, and distribution further complicate these decisions.

STATEMENTS FOR GUIDED READING

+ For many capital budgeting decisions, determination of the best choice is complicated by the fact that an additional investment in working capital is required, the replacement of already existing assets is involved, or a disinvestment is considered.

+ In evaluating investment opportunities, the minimum desired rate of return must be earned on current assets as well as on noncurrent assets.

+ When an investment opportunity requires an additional commitment to working capital, the computation of cash flows in the first and final years of the project is somewhat more complex than for other types of investment opportunities.

+ Replacement decisions are made when economic or technological factors make it possible to perform tasks at lower costs.

+ Two methods for evaluating replacement decisions are the incremental approach and the total project approach.

+ When using the incremental approach, replacement is desirable if the present value of future net cash savings is greater than the net outlay required.

+ When using the total project approach, replacement is desirable if the present value of future outflows for the proposed asset is smaller than that for the existing asset.

+ Both the incremental and the total project approaches should give the same results.

+ When considering a disinvestment decision, a firm should compare the savings desired from the use of the existing asset with the opportunity cost of its use.

+ When considering mutually exclusive alternatives, the useful lives of the proposed alternatives should be equalized for purposes of analysis.

+ Since the net present value and the internal-rate-of-return methods may yield a conflicting ranking for investment opportunities, some accountants prefer to use the profitability index to evaluate mutually exclusive alternatives.

+ The profitability index (benefit-cost ratio) is the ratio of the present value of the future cash flows to the investment required.

+ The net present value method is preferred over either the internal-rate-of-return method or the profitability index except under special circumstances.

+ A project with a higher profitability index or a higher internal rate of return should be chosen in preference to one with a higher net present value only when that choice will enable the firm to invest additional cash at a rate greater than the cost of capital <u>and</u> that investment opportunity is unavailable if the firm chooses the higher net present value project.

+ Sensitivity analysis tests to what extent decisions are affected by changes in one or more relevant factors.

+ The problems of dealing with progressive income tax rates are important for partnerships and sole proprietorships because the profits of such business firms flow through to individuals and are taxed using the rates applicable to the individuals.

+ A profit on the sale of an asset not normally resold may be a capital gain.

+ To qualify as an asset subject to the capital gains tax rate, the asset must be owned for at least one year.

+ Because of the complexity of the tax laws relating to capital gains, the firm's tax counselor should be consulted about the applicability of the capital gains tax.

+ For tax purposes, an operating loss may be carried back three years and carried forward for five years.

+ When an asset acquired by a firm qualifies for an investment tax credit, a firm may deduct directly from its tax payment for that year an amount equal to some specific percentage of the acquisition cost of this asset.

+ Social costs are those costs not borne directly by the entity making a decision and taking an action; social benefits are those benefits not accruing directly to the entity making a decision.

+ Decision making by governmental units is extremely difficult because of problems of measurement, problems of determination, and problems of distribution.

COMPREHENSION CHECK

<u>Directions</u>: Complete the following multiple-choice questions by placing the letter of the most appropriate answer available in the blank.

_____ 1. When an investment proposal requires an increase in working capital and an increase in equipment, the desired rate of return must be earned on:
   a. the working capital element of the investment.
   b. the noncurrent asset element of the investment.
   c. both of the above.

_____ 2. Investments in working capital are typically recovered:
   a. evenly throughout the life of the project.
   b. at the beginning of the project's life.
   c. at the end of the project's life.
   d. when the firm goes out of business.

_____ 3. An asset with a book value of $10,000 is sold for $7,000 cash. What is the after-tax cash effect of the sale, assuming a tax rate of 40%?
   a. an increase of $10,000
   b. an increase of $8,200
   c. an increase of $7,000
   d. an increase of $5,800

_____ 4. Sales of noncurrent assets at a loss are always desirable because they reduce taxes and increase cash flows. The preceding statement is:
a. true.
b. false.

_____ 5. Sales of noncurrent assets at a loss should always be avoided because reporting a "loss on the sale of a fixed asset" indicates mismanagement. The preceding statement is:
a. true.
b. false.

_____ 6. When comparing the total project and the incremental approaches to the analysis of investment decisions, one usually finds that:
a. the total project approach shows a higher present value for the project in question.
b. the incremental approach shows a higher present value for the project in question.
c. both approaches indicate the same decision.
d. whether both approaches indicate the same decision depends on the length of the useful life of the asset to be acquired.

_____ 7. When alternative investment opportunities have different useful lives:
a. the lives of the investment opportunities should be equalized for analysis purposes.
b. techniques do not exist to analyze the investments.
c. the appropriate analytical approach would be to assume that the longer-lived investment opportunity is sold at the end of the life of the shorter-lived opportunity.
d. the appropriate analytical approach would be to make no assumptions about the useful lives, and simply compare the net present values of each opportunity.

_____ 8. The profitability index is the ratio of:
a. the net present value to the cost of the investment.
b. the internal rate of return to the cost of capital.
c. earnings per share to the current market price of a share of the firm's stock.
d. the present value of future cash flows to the net investment cost.

_____ 9. Graduated or progressive income tax rates apply to:
a. sole proprietorships.
b. partnerships.
c. corporations.
d. individuals.

_____ 10. A four-year-old machine with an original cost of $8,000 and a book value of $1,000 is sold for $8,400. The amount of the gain on sale subject to ordinary income tax rates is:
a. $8,400.
b. $7,400.
c. $7,000.
d. $400.

_____ 11. A four-year-old machine with an original cost of $8,000 and a book value of $1,000 is sold for $8,400. The amount of gain on sale subject to the capital gains tax rate is:
a. $8,400.
b. $7,400.
c. $7,000.
d. $400.

_____ 12. An investment project with a positive net present value:
a. will have a profitability index number greater than 1.
b. will have a book rate of return greater than the minimum required return on investment.
c. will have a payback period considerably shorter than the life of the project.
d. should be accepted under all circumstances.

_____ 13. When evaluating alternative capital investment projects that have no expected future inflows (only outflows, as in the case of, perhaps, an employee-benefit project a firm has decided to undertake):
a. the net present value method is not applicable.
b. that project should be chosen that shows the highest internal rate of return.
c. that project should be chosen that shows the smallest negative net present value.
d. the profitability index numbers for all the alternatives will be positive but less than 1.

APPLICATIONS

Problem 1

A firm owns equipment with a book value of $45,000 and remaining useful life of 4 years. Annual depreciation on the equipment is $10,000 and a residual value of $5,000 is expected at the end of year 4.

A new machine with a 4-year useful life could be purchased for $70,000. The new machine would require an increase in inventory and supplies of $10,000. This increase in working capital would be recovered in cash at the end of 4 years. The new machine would cost $2,000 per year to operate. This would be an annual cash operating cost savings of $8,000. If the new machine is purchased, it would have no salvage value and would be depreciated using the straight-line method. At the present, the old equipment could be sold for $60,000 cash and any gain on such a sale would be subject to tax at the firm's normal tax rate. The firm's tax rate is 40% and its cost of capital is 18%.

```
Factors: PV of $1 when N = 3, I = 18%           = .609
         PV of $1 when N = 4, I = 18%           = .516
         PV of annuity of $1 when N = 3, I = 18% = 2.174
         PV of annuity of $1 when N = 4, I = 18% = 2.690
```

A.   Using the total project approach, determine which of the two alternatives minimizes costs.

   1. Keep old equipment.

   2. Buy new machine.

3. Compare two alternatives above.

B. Using the incremental approach determine whether or not the firm should replace the old equipment.

Problem 2

A firm is considering two mutually exclusive investment opportunities.

	Chevrolet Sedan	Mercedes
Purchase price	$8,000	$15,000
Annual cash operating costs	$900	$1,100
Expected life	3 years	6 years
Salvage value	$2,000	$3,000
Method of depreciation	straight-line	straight-line

In order to make the two investment opportunities comparable, assume that a second sedan is purchased at the end of year 3. Assume that purchase price, operating costs, life, and salvage value remain the same for the second sedan. Assume a 60% tax rate and a cost of capital of 12%.

> Factors: PV of annuity of $1 when N = 3 and I = 12% = 2.402
> PV of annuity of $1 when N = 6 and I = 12% = 4.111
> PV of $1 when N = 3 and I = 12% = .712
> PV of $1 when N = 6 and I = 12% = .507

A. Determine the present value of the cash flows associated with purchasing the Mercedes.

B.   Determine the present value of the cash flows of purchasing the two sedans:

C.   Based on the above computation, what should the firm buy? _____

FINAL COMMENTS

1.   Many students have difficulty deciding which items have tax effects and which items do not. Remember that there is no tax effect to investing in working capital. Likewise, when the working capital investment is recovered in cash at the end of the life of the investment, taxes are not affected.

2.   To compute the tax effect of selling an existing asset, first compute the gain or loss on the sale (proceeds from sale minus book value). If the selling price is greater than the book value, the difference is a gain. By applying the tax rate to the gain or loss, you can compute the tax due or the tax savings from the sale.

3.   A troublesome area for some students is the determination of the cash flow from the sale of an asset at the end of its useful life. If an investment has been depreciated down to its salvage value, the receipt of cash equal to the salvage value has no tax effect. Frequently, students will tax the salvage value forgetting that the book value of the asset is equal to that salvage value. If the asset is sold for more or less than the originally estimated salvage value, compute the tax on the gain or loss and combine it with the selling price to determine the cash flow from the final sale of the investment.

4.   The investment tax credit does <u>not</u> reduce taxable income; nor does it reduce the depreciable basis of the asset. The investment tax credit reduces the firm's taxes directly. Treating the investment credit in the same way one treats depreciation is a common mistake. Depreciation is a deduction to arrive at the amount of income that is to be taxed; the investment credit is a direct deduction from the tax that has been computed. The tax effects of the investment credit are dollar for dollar. A dollar of investment credit saves a dollar of taxes.

CHAPTER 10

RESPONSIBILITY ACCOUNTING

OVERVIEW

Responsibility accounting is the aspect of the managerial process dealing with the reporting of information to facilitate control of operations and evaluation of performance. The most formal device in the management system, a responsibility accounting system should help achieve goal congruence through positive motivation of managers. A good responsibility accounting system includes criteria for performance evaluation designed to encourage decisions that will be in the best interests of both the managers and the firm.

Segments of an entity that are identified on the basis of the managers responsible for them are called responsibility centers. Three common designations for these segments, indicating the breadth of the managers' control, are cost centers, profit centers, and investment centers.

Generally the most useful basis for evaluating managers is a comparison of budgeted and actual performances. The criteria used to evaluate individual performance should be based on the functions controlled by the manager.

The managerial hierarchy of most firms is arranged in either a vertical or a horizontal structure. With a vertical structure, much responsibility is assigned to the highest levels of management, and responsibility is said to be centralized. In a horizontal structure, many types of responsibility are assigned to managers at the lower levels, and responsibility is said to be decentralized.

While managers should be held responsible for only those costs over which they can exercise control, such is not always the case in practice. Often costs in one department are allocated to other departments. Transfer prices, devices often used to create artificial profit centers, are akin to allocations. It should be remembered that allocations and transfer prices are managerial accounting devices, and although they may be changed, these changes do not affect the total income of the firm so long as the behavior of the managers of the individual segments remains unchanged.

STATEMENTS FOR GUIDED READING

+ The function of responsibility accounting is to report information to facilitate control of operations and to evaluate performance.

+ As a part of the total management system, a responsibility accounting system should assist in goal congruence, managers working in harmony toward the goals and objectives of the firm.

+ Since performance measurement systems tend to motivate managers to focus their efforts in relation to the criteria used for their evaluations, careful selection of evaluation criteria is extremely important in order to serve the best interests of the managers and of the firm.

+ As a part of a responsibility accounting system, performance reports keep managers informed of their progress in meeting the criteria by which they are being judged; the focus of these reports should be the functions over which the managers have control.

+ Despite the interdependency of a firm's managers, each manager's sphere of responsibility should be defined as clearly as possible.

+ Responsibility centers are segments of the activities of an entity identified on the basis of the managers responsible for them.

+ Cost centers, profit centers, and investment centers are the names of three types of responsibility centers; these names indicate the breadth of control assigned the manager.

+ The manager of a cost center is responsible for controlling the costs incurred by that center.

+ The manager of a profit center is responsible for controlling both costs and revenues of that center.

+ The sales of a natural profit center are to external markets; the sales of artificial profit centers are primarily to internal markets, and the selling price for these sales is called the transfer price.

+ The manager of an investment center is responsible for controlling the costs, the revenues, and the investments of that center.

+ Generally, the most useful basis for evaluating the performance of managers is a comparison of budgeted and actual performances.

+ Vertical structure and horizontal structure are two basic approaches to the organization of the managerial hierarchy of a firm.

+ Vertical structure is centralized; much of the responsibility for control is assigned to the higher management levels.

+ Horizontal structure is decentralized; much of the responsibility for control is assigned to the lower management levels.

+ Despite the theoretical desirability of having managers held responsible for only those costs over which they can exercise control, in practice there are tendencies to allocate (1) costs controlled at one level to all the cost centers at a lower level and (2) costs of service departments to operating departments.

+ Cost allocations are almost invariably arbitrary, and the bias inherent in the allocation method selected can have serious behavioral consequences.

+ When _actual_ costs are prorated based on the number of hours of service, the managers of the service departments may not be motivated to fulfill their responsibilities efficiently because they know that all costs they incur will be spread over the operating departments; with this method, the managers of operating departments tend to underuse services.

+ When service charges are based on a fixed amount regardless of actual use, the managers of operating departments tend to overuse the service.

+ A per-hour rate based on the cost of obtaining a service from an outside source may be difficult to determine and the charge may be so high that operating managers would underuse the service.

+ Of the four common methods of charging operating departments for the costs of a service department, the method combining budgeted variable costs and budgeted fixed costs is best under most circumstances since current inefficiencies of the service department are not passed on to the operating departments, and the resultant service charge may encourage necessary use and discourage overuse.

+ The total income of a firm is unaffected by changes in allocations and transfer prices unless such changes induce managers to alter their operations in some way.

COMPREHENSION CHECK

Directions: Complete the following multiple-choice questions by placing the letter of the most appropriate answer available in the blank.

_____ 1. Responsibility accounting:
   a. produces goal congruence.
   b. has been mandated by the federal government.
   c. is the most formal communication device in the military-industrial complex.
   d. is that aspect of the managerial process dealing with the reporting of information to facilitate control of operations and evaluation of performance.

_____ 2. Ideally, a responsibility accounting system:
   a. encourages managers to focus on a single measure of evaluation.
   b. generates reports for managers to show how well they are doing in relation to performance criteria.
   c. causes managers to eliminate interdependence.
   d. gives top management a method for eliminating interdependence.

_____ 3. Responsibility centers identify segments of an entity on the basis of:
   a. the managers responsible for them.
   b. geographical area.
   c. product taxes.
   d. specific products.

_____ 4. Cost centers are segments on which:
   a. cost accountants prepare reports.
   b. a few people perform one or several operations on a product.
   c. managers are responsible for costs incurred but are not responsible for revenues.
   d. managers are responsible for controlling both costs and revenues.

_____ 5. A natural profit center:
   a. sells its output at transfer prices.
   b. should use incremental profits as the major criterion for performance evaluation.
   c. operates in external markets.
   d. earns revenues "naturally."

_____ 6. Generally, the most useful basis for evaluating managers is a comparison of:
   a. budgeted and actual performance.
   b. one segment in relation to other segments.
   c. budgeted and actual revenues.
   d. budgeted and actual expenditures.

_____ 7. In a vertical organizational structure:
   a. responsibilities at the lower levels of management are relatively broad.
   b. responsibility is decentralized.
   c. responsibility is centralized with the greatest responsibility assigned to middle management.
   d. responsibility is assigned to the highest levels of management.

_____ 8. In a set of reports designed for a firm with vertical structure, the amount of detail:
   a. should increase as the reports go to the higher levels of the hierarchy.
   b. should be sufficient to indicate the performance of all subordinates of the managers receiving a particular report.
   c. should highlight problem areas in order for all managers to initiate corrective action.
   d. drops as the reports ascend the hierarchy.

_____ 9. The tendency to allocate costs controllable at one level to all cost centers at a lower level reflects:
   a. an objective of cost accounting.
   b. an objective of managerial accounting.
   c. the need to conform to federal regulation.
   d. a basic tenet of responsibility accounting.

_____ 10. The tendency to allocate costs of service departments to operating departments:
   a. is supported by a needs argument.
   b. is supported by a benefits argument.
   c. ensures that managers are aware of their controllable costs.
   d. engenders reports in which service departments are natural profit centers.

_____ 11. When the actual costs of a service department are allocated to the operating departments based on the number of hours of service performed in each department, operating managers:
   a. tend to overuse the service.
   b. tend to underuse the service.
   c. shift the inefficiencies of their departments to the service department.
   d. shift the inefficiencies of their departments to the active operating departments.

_____ 12. When the costs of a service department are allocated to the operating departments in a fixed amount regardless of the use of the service, operating managers:
   a. tend to underuse the service.
   b. are encouraged to use the service.
   c. shift the inefficiencies of their departments to the active operating departments.
   d. attempt to transfer these costs to other service departments.

_____ 13. If allocations of service department costs are to be made to operating departments, charges should reflect:
   a. use of other operating departments.
   b. actual costs rather than budgeted costs.
   c. the quality of service.
   d. budgeted costs rather than actual costs.

_____ 14. As managerial accounting devices, changes in allocations and transfer prices:
   a. directly affect the total income of the firm.
   b. may induce managers to change their operations and thereby change total income of the firm.
   c. are a sign of an inefficient operation.
   c. are a sign of an efficient operation.

APPLICATIONS

Problem 1

Barkman Company has one service department and two operating divisions. The service department, the computer center, incurred the following costs for 1979:

Variable costs	$31,250
Fixed costs	61,200
Total	$92,450

Budgeted costs for the computer center were $12 per hour of use plus $60,000.

During 1979, Lee Division used the computer center 1,000 hours although they had estimated their use of the service center at 1,200 hours. During that year, Grant Division used the computer center 1,500 hours although they had projected their use at 1,400 hours.

A. Allocate computer costs to operating divisions based on actual number of hours of use.

Costs allocated to Lee Division = $_____

Costs allocated to Grant Division = $_____

B. Allocate computer costs to operating divisions based on a use charge of $36.00 per hour, $12 per hour to cover variable costs and $24 per hour to cover fixed costs.

Costs allocated to Lee Division = $_____

Costs allocated to Grant Division = $_____

C.   Allocate budgeted fixed computer costs to the operating divisions based on expected use, and allocate $12 to computer cost for every hour of use.

Costs allocated to Lee Division:

Fixed costs	$_____
Variable costs	$_____
Total	$_____

Costs allocated to Grant Division:

Fixed costs	$_____
Variable costs	$_____
Total	$_____

Problem 2

Heather Corporation is organized horizontally with two decentralized profit centers.

Center A produces a subassembly which is sold to Center B for $230 each. A has a plant capacity of 1,000 units and produces at this level. All of A's output is sold to B. B takes the subassembly and incorporates it into the final product which is sold to outsiders for $600 each.

A's cost structure consists of variable costs of $90 a unit plus fixed costs of $120,000. B's costs include the cost of the subassemblies plus an additional variable cost per unit of $300 and fixed costs of $10,000.

A.   What is the transfer price? $_____

B.   Is the $230 cost to Center B considered to be a variable cost, a mixed cost, or a fixed cost?

C.   Prepare income statements using the contribution margin approach for Center A, Center B, and Heather Corporation assuming 1,000 units were produced and sold.

Center A
Income Statement
for One Year

Sales	$_____
Variable costs	$_____
Contribution margin	$_____
Fixed costs	$_____
Income	$_____

Center B
Income Statement
for One Year

Sales	$_____
Variable costs	$_____
Contribution margin	$_____
Fixed costs	$_____
Income	$_____

Heather Corporation
Income Statement
for One Year

Sales	$_____
Variable costs	$_____
Contribution margin	$_____
Fixed costs	$_____
Income	$_____

CHAPTER 11

DIVISIONAL PERFORMANCE MEASUREMENT

OVERVIEW

This chapter deals with some aspects of responsibility accounting in investment centers. (You will remember that investment centers are segments the managers of which have responsibility for profit and a return on investment.) Decentralization and its benefits are considered in somewhat more detail than in Chapter 10.

Return on investment and residual income are introduced as commonly used divisional performance measures, and the complications of measuring divisional profit and divisional investment are discussed. Division managers are confronted with many of the same types of decisions as were discussed in Chapters 7-9 and with the need for transfer prices as discussed in Chapter 10. Analytical tools for handling decisions are included in this chapter.

Divisional performance reports have been interpreted in two ways: as reports on the performance of the division, and as reports on the performance of the division's manager. The chapter suggests that these interpretations use different standards for comparison.

The chapter concludes with an analysis of the behavioral problems connected with the use of various performance evaluation criteria, emphasizing, as in Chapter 10, the need to use criteria that will encourage managers to follow courses of action beneficial to the firm as a whole. Finally, the merits of various methods of transfer pricing are discussed.

STATEMENTS FOR GUIDED READING

+ Decentralized firms make extensive use of investment centers, with managers having responsibility for profit and return on investment.

+ Decentralization enables managers at lower levels to resolve conflicts and helps top management to apply the principle of management by exception.

+ Divisional profit, the net result of all revenue and expense items controllable by the manager, should be used to evaluate a division.

+ Return on investment is income divided by investment.

+ An expansion of the return-on-investment formula is the return-on-sales ratio multiplied by the investment turnover.

+ The amount of income that a division produces in excess of the minimum desired rate of return for the firm is its residual income.

+ Residual income is income minus the product of investment multiplied by the desired return on investment.

+ When there are costs and assets joint to two or more divisions, allocation or assignment to the divisions may be arbitrary, causing disagreement among division managers.

+ The use of liabilities in the computation of divisional investment will cause the return on investment to increase.

+ Possible bases for the valuation of fixed assets include original cost, original cost less accumulated depreciation, and current replacement cost of fixed assets.

+ Original cost less accumulated depreciation is the most popular approach for determining the value of assets to be assigned to the divisions.

+ Some bases for comparison of divisional results are comparison among divisions of the same firm, comparison with historical results in the same division, comparison with industry averages, and comparison with budgets.

+ The use of return on investment as the criterion for divisional performance evaluation may cause managers to pass up projects with a promised return of less than the return on investment currently earned by the division.

+ Lower income in earlier years and the natural tendency of return on investment to rise as the book value of the investment falls are two major factors which discourage managers when they consider substantial investments.

+ The transfer pricing policy of a firm is of critical importance in divisional performance evaluation because these prices influence revenues of the selling division and costs of the buying division.

+ Transfer at market prices is generally considered the best transfer pricing policy.

COMPREHENSION CHECK

Directions: Complete the following statements by writing a word or phrase in the blanks.

1. A _____ firm makes extensive use of investment centers.

2. Top management can apply the principle of management by _____ when a firm is decentralized.

3. Divisional profit is the net result of revenue and expense items _____ by the division manager.

4. Total _____ of all divisions may exceed the total income of the firm.

5. Income divided by investment is _____ _____ _____.

6. The return-on-sales ratio is _____ divided by sales.

7. Sales divided by investment is the _____ _____.

8. A measure of the amount of income a division produces in excess of the minimum desired _____ _____ _____ is the residual income.

9. Residual income is income minus the product of _____ multiplied by the desired return on investment.

10. Because of unallocated costs and unassigned assets, it is not only possible but necessary that the divisions earn considerably more than the minimum desired _____ _____ _____ in order for the firm as a whole to do so.

11. Using any _____ in the determination of divisional investment will naturally cause the return on investment of the divisions to increase.

12. The most popular valuation base for fixed assets is _____ _____ _____ _____ _____.

13. _____ start-up costs over several years is an approach that might encourage managers to pursue worthwhile investments.

14. The transfer pricing method generally considered the best is a policy of transfer at _____ _____.

APPLICATIONS

Problem 1

A budgeted income statement for 1980 for Mirror Division of Solar Products follows:

Sales	$16.00 × 3,000 units	$48,000
Variable costs	9.00 × 3,000 units	27,000
Contribution margin		21,000
Fixed costs		11,000
Divisional profit		$10,000

Division investment = $80,000
Minimum desired return on investment = 10%.

Compute:

1. Return on investment (ROI) = _____

   divided by _____ = _____ %

2. The minimum amount of divisional profit required in order to meet the minimum desired

   ROI = $_____ × _____ or $_____

3. Residual income = _____ - _____ = $_____

4. Return on sales = $_____ ÷ _____ = _____ %

5. Investment turnover = _____ ÷ _____ = _____ times

6. Mirror Division could sell an additional 1,500 units at $16 each in 1980. Variable costs per unit would be $10 on these additional units. Fixed costs would increase by $6,000. An additional investment of $40,000 would be required.
   a. Determine the change in divisional profit if the additional 1,500 units are sold.

Incremental revenue	$ _____
Incremental variable costs	_____
Incremental contribution margin	_____
Incremental fixed costs	_____
Incremental divisional profit	$ _____

   b. If the additional 1,500 units are sold, what would be the residual income?

   $ _____

   c. Should the 1,500 units be sold?   _____

Problem 2

   Wood Division currently has a return on investment of 23%; profits are $103,500 and investment in the division is $450,000. The manager of Wood Division refused the following investment opportunities because each would have lowered his return on investment.

	Amount of Investment	Annual Profit
Alpha	$100,000	$14,000
Beta	50,000	8,000
Sigma	23,000	4,000
Omega	17,000	1,530
Phi	33,400	4,000
Psi	72,000	14,400
Pi	38,000	6,080
Delta	14,500	2,000
Chi	6,800	800

If top management wants each division to maximize residual income instead of return on investment, which of the above investment opportunities should have been accepted by the manager of Wood Division? Minimum desired rate of return is 14%.

Problem 3

For each of the following cases, fill in the blanks. The minimum desired rate of return is 10%.

	Case I	Case II	Case III
Sales	$_____	$ 40,000	$_____
Income	$_____	$_____	$ 9,000
Investment turnover	2 times	_____ times	_____ times
Return on sales	_____ %	10 %	4 %
Return on investment	_____ %	20 %	9 %
Investment	$ 50,000	$_____	$_____
Residual income	$ 1,000	$_____	$_____

Problem 4

Master Corporation has three decentralized divisions; Mini, Micro, and Maxi. Maxi Division purchases the total output of Mini and Micro. Maxi combines 1 unit of output of Mini (called a mini) and 3 units of output of Micro (each unit is called a micro) into a finished unit. Current partial income statements appear as follows:

	Divisions		
	Mini	Micro	Maxi
Sales 500 minis @ $38	$19,000		
Sales 1,500 micros @ $12		$18,000	
Sales 500 units @ $150			$75,000
Variable costs	10,000	13,500	58,000
Contribution margin	$ 9,000	$ 4,500	$17,000

The market price of a mini is currently $40 and the market price of a micro is $15. The division managers of Micro and Mini have just informed the manager of Maxi that they are going to increase the transfer price to the current market price.

A. Recast the partial income statements of Mini, Micro, and Maxi based on the new transfer price.

	Divisions		
	Mini	Micro	Maxi
Sales			
Variable costs			
Contribution margin			

B. Prepare a partial income statement (down to contribution margin) for Master Corporation.

Sales

Variable costs

Contribution margin

CHAPTER 12

CONTROL AND EVALUATION OF COST CENTERS

OVERVIEW

Performance evaluation of both profit and investment centers has been discussed in previous chapters. A technique exists which aids in control and performance evaluation for those cost centers that involve production of an identifiable and measurable product. The technique is called standard costing, and the cost centers to which it applies are, for the most part, individual operating departments in a manufacturing firm. This chapter covers the development of standard costs and the ways they can be helpful in budgeting and in performance evaluation.

The use of standard costs necessitates determining a standard or norm for both the price of an input factor (something used to produce a product) and the quantity that <u>should</u> be used in the process of producing a unit of output (the product). If such standards can be established, variances from budgets can be analyzed in more detail, which is important for fixing responsibility for variances, in keeping with the concept of responsibility accounting.

The chapter discusses different methods of setting standards and details for computing variances based on whatever standards are established. The chapter also presents some suggestions for interpreting the newly computed variances and repeats a comment made several times already in this text (though in different contexts): great care must be taken in interpreting the results in one part of a firm because actions of one manager can affect the results shown in a report to another manager.

QUESTIONS FOR GUIDED READING

+   What is the difference between effectiveness and efficiency?

+   What is a standard?

+   What are the two aspects of a standard for efficiency?

+   How are standard costs and budgets related?

+   In the computation of a total standard cost per unit, is the standard based on inputs or outputs?

+   For what basic variable costs are standards established?

+   What is meant by standard labor hours allowed?

+   What are the two components of standard cost of labor per unit of product?

+   What two variances can be computed when a firm establishes a standard labor cost per unit of product?

+ What condition determines whether a variance is favorable or unfavorable?

+ On what two different bases can you compute a flexible budget allowance for a variable cost for which you have developed a standard?

+ What two variances can be computed when a firm establishes a standard variable overhead cost per unit of product?

+ Why is the variable overhead efficiency variance likely to coincide in direction with the labor efficiency variance?

+ In what way is the computation of material variances different from the computation of variances for other variable costs?

+ What is meant by the interaction effects incorporated in cost variances?

+ How can actions or decisions by one manager affect cost variances reported by other managers?

+ When should a variance be investigated?

+ What are control charts?

+ Are favorable variances always good?

+ What approaches are available for establishing standards?

+ Should standards be based on ideal conditions, current conditions, historical performance, or something else?

+ When should standards be revised?

+ What factors should be considered when including standard cost variances in performance reports?

+ Can fixed costs best be controlled by using standards?

+ How should fixed costs be handled in performance reports?

+ What problems arise in analyzing variances for overhead items that contain both fixed and variable components?

+ Are standard costs useful for nonmanufacturing activities?

COMPREHENSION CHECK

Directions: For each of the following multiple-choice questions, place the letter of the most appropriate answer in the space provided.

_____ 1. Which of the following is true?
        a. The most effective means of doing something is usually the most efficient.
        b. The most efficient means of doing something is usually the most effective.
        c. The effectiveness of a procedure depends on its efficiency.
        d. None of the above is true.

_____   2.   Standards for efficiency must take into consideration:
    a.   input.
    b.   output.
    c.   both input and output.
    d.   either input or output but not both.

_____   3.   Flexible budget allowances are most appropriate for:
    a.   variable costs.
    b.   fixed costs.
    c.   joint costs.
    d.   opportunity costs.

_____   4.   A total standard cost per unit incorporates all of the following except:
    a.   standard prices for input factors.
    b.   standard quantities for input factors.
    c.   standard variances for input factors.
    d.   standard costs for output.

_____   5.   The standard number of labor hours allowed in a given period is:
    a.   total labor hours worked times the standard cost per hour.
    b.   total number of units produced times the standard number of labor hours
         required for a unit of product.
    c.   total number of labor hours that can be paid for with the total labor budget
         for the period.
    d.   budgeted labor hours times the standard cost per labor hour.

_____   6.   Which of the following calculations would give the cost variance related to price?
    a.   actual quantity of input × (actual cost of a unit of input - standard cost
         of a unit of input)
    b.   (actual quantity of input × standard cost of a unit of input) - (standard
         quantity of input required for actual quantity of output × standard cost of
         a unit of input)
    c.   actual selling price of quantity produced - budgeted selling price of quantity
         produced
    d.   (quantity of output produced - quantity of input used) × standard cost of a
         unit of input

_____   7.   A flexible budget allowance can be computed based on:
    a.   the actual quantity used of an input factor.
    b.   the actual quantity of output produced.
    c.   both a and b.
    d.   either a or b but not both.

_____   8.   When analyzing variable overhead, the equivalent of the labor rate variance is:
    a.   the spending variance.
    b.   the efficiency variance.
    c.   the use variance.
    d.   the volume variance.

_____   9.   The computation of a material price variance is somewhat different from the compu-
              tation of other price variances because:
    a.   a company may buy its material from several different suppliers.
    b.   the quantity of materials purchased is not always equal to the standard quan-
         tity required for production that period.
    c.   discounts may be earned from purchasing materials in large quantities.
    d.   the quantity of materials purchased is not usually equal to the quantity of
         materials used for production that period.

_____ 10. A problem that arises in interpreting price and use variances is that:
    a. once they have been isolated they must be investigated.
    b. the result of a decision that produces a favorable variance in one department may be an unfavorable variance in some other department.
    c. the managers responsible for the variances may not agree with the standards.
    d. there is little that a manager has left to do because the causes of the variances are clear from the computations.

_____ 11. Which of the following is true?
    a. Unfavorable variances are the result of poor standards.
    b. Favorable variances need not be investigated because they indicate that things are going better than had been planned.
    c. Unfavorable variances are more likely when standards are set using engineering methods.
    d. Control charts will show limit lines within which neither favorable nor unfavorable variances will be investigated.

_____ 12. A major drawback to the use of past (historical) performance in the establishment of standards is that:
    a. such standards perpetuate past inefficiencies.
    b. the past has no relevance to the future.
    c. such standards are not likely to be attainable currently.
    d. such standards produce fewer unfavorable variances.

_____ 13. When performance reports are prepared and standard costs are used:
    a. some variances for variable cost items may not be reported to managers of operating departments using the input factor for which there is a variance.
    b. noncontrollable costs should be included if they are greater than the controllable costs.
    c. only unfavorable variances should be reported so that managers can concentrate on correcting things that went wrong.
    d. none of the above.

_____ 14. If the budget (cost prediction) formula for an element (or all) of overhead includes both a fixed and a variable component:
    a. only a total budget variance can be computed.
    b. any variance must be related to the variable component.
    c. the variance related to the fixed component should be computed separately and reported to a level of management above that at which the cost occurred.
    d. only the variance related to the variable component should be computed and reported.

APPLICATIONS

<u>Problem 1</u>

The major product of the Magic Company is the Trix, the standard variable cost of which is as follows:

Material:	
3 yds. of Quick at $2.80 per yd.	$ 8.40
8 yds. of Aye at $1.50 per yd.	12.00
Labor:	
2 hrs. of smoothing labor at $6.50 per hr.	13.00
1/2 hr. of packing labor at $4.00 per hr.	2.00
Variable overhead at $7.00 per labor hr.	17.50
Total	$52.90

The company has decided to use a new material, Wink, in place of Aye in the production of Trix. Wink is less expensive (expected price is $1.20 per yard), and the final product is just as good as the product now being produced. Carefully controlled tests of the new material have shown that a unit of Trix would require 9 yards of Wink and a half yard more of Quik. Because of Wink's fabric content, smoothing labor would be reduced by a half-hour, but its bulkiness increases the difficulty of packing so that packing labor would be increased by a half-hour.

Compute a new standard cost for a unit of Trix, based on the decision to substitute Wink for Aye.

<u>Problem 2</u>

The standard variable cost of a single unit of Product Q is as follows:

Material X	6 lbs. @ $1 per lb.	$6.00
Material Y	.5 gals. @ $4.80 per gal.	2.40
Mixing labor	1/2 hr. @ $7.20 per hr.	3.60
Variable overhead	$10 per hr. of mixing labor	5.00
Total variable standard cost per unit of Q		$17.00

The firm that makes product Q (its only product) expects to make 25,000 units of Q during 19X7.

A.   What are the expected costs for 19X7 for:

1.   Material X? $_____

2.   Material Y? $_____

3. Mixing labor? $_____

4. Variable overhead? $_____

B. During 19X7, the firm actually produces 23,800 units of Q and incurs costs as follows:

Purchases of material X, all used immediately in production of Q
   142,500 lbs. at $1.04 per lb. $148,200
Purchases of material Y, of which all but 2,200 gallons were
used in production of Q
   14,200 gals. at $4.75 per gal.   67,450
Mixing labor
   11,700 hrs. at $7.15 per hr.   83,655
Variable overhead   119,300

1. What material price variance was incurred in connection with
    material X for the year? $_____

2. What material price variance was incurred in connection with
    Material Y for the year? $_____

3. What material use variance was incurred in connection with
    Material X for the year? $_____

4. What material use variance was incurred in connection with
    Material Y for the year? $_____

5. What labor rate variance was incurred during the year? $_____

6. What labor efficiency variance was incurred during the year? $_____

7. What is the variable overhead spending variance for the year? $_____

8. What is the variable overhead efficiency variance for the year? $_____

FINAL COMMENTS

The chapter shows several ways of computing variances, including the use of formulas. Many students concentrate on learning the formulas and then lose sight of what they are trying to accomplish. Consequently, they are never sure whether a variance is favorable or unfavorable, or what should be subtracted from what in a given formula. Remember that you are trying to determine whether performance (actual results) was better or worse than planned, and that standards represent plans. Thinking, rather than memorizing formulas, is your best bet. For example, if a firm pays a higher price than it had planned for materials, the variance is unfavorable and equal to the difference in price times the quantity of material purchased. If a firm pays a lower price than planned for its laborers, the variance is favorable and equal to the difference in price times the number of labor hours used. If workers worked more hours than considered necessary for the number of units actually finished, the variance is unfavorable (the workers took too long). Try to describe each situation in common sense terms.

CHAPTER 13

VARIABLE AND ABSORPTION COSTING, AND STANDARD FIXED COSTS

OVERVIEW

This chapter introduces product costing, the calculation of unit costs for inventory valuation and income determination. The two principal methods of product costing are variable costing and absorption costing. Variable costing conforms to the contribution margin format of the income statement, which approach has been recommended throughout this book for its usefulness in planning and control. Absorption costing requires the use of a fixed cost per unit so as to arrive at a total per-unit cost for the purpose of inventory determination. Absorption costing is required for external financial reporting and income tax purposes. The drawbacks of dealing with a unit cost that includes fixed costs have been mentioned often in earlier chapters.

Depending on the relationship between sales and production, the two costing methods, variable and absorption, can produce differing amounts of income. A standard fixed cost per unit is often computed for product costing purposes, but this amount is not useful for planning and control. Related to the concept of a standard per-unit fixed cost is the idea of a predetermined rate for fixed manufacturing overhead. Both standard per-unit fixed costs and predetermined overhead rates can be useful in preventing misinterpretations of absorption costing income statements.

STATEMENTS FOR GUIDED READING

+ The use of a fixed cost per unit is unwise for managerial purposes but is required for financial reporting and income tax purposes.

+ Under both variable and absorption costing, the product cost per unit is limited to manufacturing costs, with selling and administrative costs being expensed in the period incurred.

+ The salient feature of variable costing is the exclusion of any fixed manufacturing costs from the determination of unit costs for inventory purposes.

+ Variable costing employs the basic format of the contribution margin income statement.

+ Both variable costing and absorption costing can use either actual or standard costs.

+ Under actual absorption costing, the fixed cost per unit of product will depend on the level of production and can therefore change from period to period.

+ Income under absorption costing is affected by the quantity of product produced as well as by the quantity of product sold. Income under variable costing is not affected by the amount produced.

+ Income under absorption costing will be higher than under variable costing when production is greater than sales, and vice versa.

+ The difference between absorption and variable costing incomes is equal to the difference between fixed costs in the beginning and ending inventories.

+ Many firms use a standard fixed cost per unit instead of calculating actual fixed cost per unit each period.

+ The standard fixed cost per unit is "applied" to units of product, and firms that use a standard fixed cost per unit will usually have either overapplied or underapplied fixed manufacturing overhead.

+ A principal advantage of using a standard fixed cost per unit is that the effect of production on income is isolated in a figure called the volume variance.

+ Multiple-product firms find it useful to set standard fixed costs through the intermediate step of calculating a predetermined overhead rate for fixed costs, based on some input factor such as direct labor hours or machine-hours.

+ A major advantage of variable costing for managerial purposes is that it presents information in a form suitable for volume-cost-profit analysis.

+ Variable costing does not require allocations of fixed costs to units of product.

+ Variable costing may encourage a short-term outlook, with managers being tempted to set prices too low to cover all costs and still earn profits.

COMPREHENSION CHECK

Directions: Draw a line through the number of each false statement.

1. Absorption costing inventory will usually be lower than variable costing inventory.

2. If inventory is increasing, absorption costing income will be higher than variable costing income.

3. Under variable costing, all variable costs are included in inventory.

4. Standard fixed costs are not relevant for planning and control.

5. Absorption costing must be used for financial reporting and income tax accounting.

6. Overapplied (or underapplied) fixed overhead consists of two components—a budget variance and a volume variance.

7. Predetermined overhead rates are based on budgeted fixed overhead and some measure of activity like direct labor hours.

8. A principal advantage of using standard fixed costs rather than actual fixed costs is that income will be affected only by sales, not by production.

9. A firm that shows consistently favorable volume variances is probably operating very efficiently.

10. Inadequate control over fixed costs usually shows up as an unfavorable budget variance.

11. One basic difference between variable costing and absorption costing is in their treatments of variable selling and administrative costs.

12. A firm that uses absorption costing and sells fewer units than budgeted will have an unfavorable volume variance.

13. Absorption costing is incompatible with the contribution margin format of the income statement.

14. You do not need to know the quantity of product manufactured to prepare an income statement using variable costing.

15. A period cost is one that is expensed when incurred.

16. Inventoriable costs are usually called product costs.

17. If a firm using absorption costing maintains a constant level of inventory, its reported incomes will be equal to variable costing incomes.

18. Use of a standard per-unit fixed cost assists in predicting levels of costs to be incurred.

19. The selection of an activity level to use in determining a standard per-unit fixed cost has important effects on the operations of the firm.

20. Because absorption costing includes all of the firm's costs as costs of product, managers responsible for pricing would not be tempted to set selling prices too low.

APPLICATIONS

Problem 1 Variable and Absorption Costing

The Miller Company makes a single product. Data are given below.

Selling price	$20
Variable production costs	$8
Variable selling costs	$1
Annual fixed costs:	
Production	$240,000
Selling	$300,000

The firm began 19X8 with no inventory, produced 100,000 units, and sold 80,000. Prepare income statements for 19X8 using variable costing and absorption costing.

Problem 2 Predetermined Overhead Rates

The Ralston Company makes two principal products, relevant data about which are as follows:

	Product	
	X	Y
Selling price	$10	$20
Variable production costs	$3	$12
Direct labor hours required, per unit	.5	1.0

Total annual fixed production costs are $100,000, selling and administrative costs are $220,000. In 19X8 the firm had the following results.

	X	Y
Production	40,000	25,000
Sales	35,000	25,000

There were no beginning inventories and all costs were incurred as expected, except that actual fixed production costs were $98,500.

A.   Determine the standard fixed cost per unit for each product based on normal activity of 50,000 direct labor hours per year.

B.   Prepare an income statement for 19X8, showing any variances as deductions from standard cost of goods sold.

FINAL COMMENTS

1.   Variable and absorption costing are approaches to determining the cost of units <u>on hand</u>. Hence, unit costs under neither method would include selling and administrative costs. Such costs are expenses in the period incurred and are not inventoriable costs.

2.   Be sure you understand the difference between production costs <u>incurred</u> and cost of goods sold. Both variable and absorption costing consider on-hand units as assets; the critical difference between the methods is in their recognition of fixed costs. Absorption costing considers fixed costs as inventoriable; variable costing does not. What is or is not inventoriable is an accounting issue, not a matter of fact. The production costs that are incurred are the same regardless of which costing method is adopted.

3.   The volume variance relates only to fixed production costs and depends on production, not sales. It is an unfailing sign of standard absorption costing! It arises only because actual production (in units or in labor hours) was not the same as the production level used to set the standard fixed cost.

CHAPTER 14

PRODUCT COSTING: PROCESS, JOB ORDER, STANDARD

OVERVIEW

This chapter continues the discussion and illustration of product costing, the assignment of costs for inventory purposes. Manufacturing costs flow through three major inventory accounts: raw materials, goods in process, and finished goods. An inventory amount must be calculated for each inventory account, and a cost must be determined for inventory items leaving the entity, because such costs affect the cost of goods sold, and the firm's income.

As in Chapter 13, both actual and standard costing are considered, the latter being advocated whenever possible because of its advantages for control.

Product costing is also treated from the standpoint of the type of manufacturing operation being performed. Firms that produce relatively homogeneous products in continuous processes use a form of process costing. Complications arise with the costing of semifinished units in a process costing firm, and the concept of a "unit of product" must be refined to cover the idea of an "equivalent unit."

Firms that produce single, high-value products (such as buildings or printing presses) or identifiable batches of unique products made to customer order use some form of job order costing. Predetermined overhead rates for individual departments are particularly useful in such firms.

STATEMENTS FOR GUIDED READING

+ Manufacturing firms have three kinds of inventory: raw materials, work in process, and finished goods.

+ Two types of cost accounting systems that reflect a firm's type of operation are process costing and job order costing.

+ Process costing is used by firms that manufacture the same product again and again in a more or less continuous process.

+ Job order costing is used by firms that manufacture products to customer order, making them in separate, identifiable batches.

+ Standard costing can be used by some job order firms and by nearly any process costing firm.

+ Standard costing is especially desirable for a multiple-product firm.

+ A major advantage of standard costing is that it gives managers timely information about variances.

+ Under any cost accounting system, costs flow into a Work in Process account, then into a Finished Goods Inventory account, and, finally, into an account for Cost of Goods Sold.

+ Process costing firms must calculate a figure called <u>equivalent</u> <u>production</u>.

+ Process costing may be used with first-in-first-out or weighted average methods of recognizing cost flows.

+ A problem that confronts firms with several sequential processes is the need to calculate a unit cost for each process separately.

+ Job order cost firms generally charge jobs with actual material and labor costs while using a predetermined rate to apply overhead to each job.

+ Job order costing requires considerably more recordkeeping than process costing and is therefore more expensive to maintain.

COMPREHENSION CHECK

<u>Directions</u>: Draw a line through the number of each false statement.

1. A firm that uses standard process costing will have equivalent production different from one that uses actual process costing.

2. General Motors Corporation probably uses job order costing because it makes so many different models of automobiles.

3. A firm that uses standard costing will show lower incomes than one using actual costing because the former will show all variances as expenses.

4. The calculation of equivalent production under the weighted average method does not require knowledge of the number of units in the beginning inventory.

5. Both weighted average and first-in-first-out equivalent production can be effectively used for control purposes.

6. Manufacturing firms usually have three types of inventory.

7. It costs more to maintain a job order costing system than a process costing system.

8. A manufacturer of bread would be more likely to use a form of process costing than a form of job order costing.

9. The materials price variance is normally isolated when materials are put into process.

10. Firms that use job order costing cannot use standard costs.

11. Firms that use job order costing will rarely have a volume variance.

12. The use of standard process costing eliminates the need to calculate equivalent production.

13. In a firm that uses process costing, the calculation of cost per unit under the weighted average method employs both costs incurred during the current period and costs in the beginning inventory.

14. A firm using job order costing will probably charge jobs with actual costs for materials, labor, and overhead.

15. The cost of ending work in process inventory is the calculated unit cost multiplied by the number of equivalent units on hand.

16. Standard cost of goods sold can be calculated without knowing production for the period.

17. Both actual and standard absorption costing are acceptable for financial reporting purposes.

APPLICATIONS

Problem 1 Job Order Costing

The York Vault Company makes large bank vaults to customer order. During March of 19X6 the firm worked on two vaults, designated as jobs M-1 and M-2. Data are:

	M-1	M-2
Materials used on jobs	$ 65,000	$ 74,000
Direct labor	$210,000	$180,000

Overhead is charged at $7.50 per direct labor hour. The wage rate for all workers is $5 per hour. Total overhead incurred in March was $600,000, which equaled the amount budgeted. Job M-1 was completed in March and sold for $810,000. Job M-2 was also completed in March, but was not sold until early April. Selling and administrative expenses for March were $87,000.

A. Determine the total costs to be charged to each job.

B.   Prepare an income statement for March.

Problem 2   Process Costing, Unit Costs

The following data summarize the results of June 19X5 for the MEL Company.

Beginning inventory in units, 60% complete	2,000
Units completed during June	24,000
Ending inventory, 40% complete	4,000
Cost data:	
Beginning inventory	$14,410
Incurred during June	$295,350

Determine the cost per unit using the weighted average method and the dollar amount of ending inventory of work in process.

Problem 3   Standard Costing

The standard cost of the Jackson Company's one product is given below.

Materials 2 gals. at $.50	$ 1.00
Direct labor 1/2 hr. at $6	3.00
Variable overhead $8 per direct labor hour	4.00
Fixed overhead	2.00
Total standard cost	$10.00

The standard fixed cost per unit is based on budgeted monthly costs of $40,000 and normal activity of 20,000 units per month. Transactions for July 19X5 are given below.

1.	Material purchases	40,000 gals. at $.50	$20,000
2.	Material use	36,700 gals.	
3.	Direct labor	9,100 hrs. at $6	$54,600
4.	Variable overhead incurred		$74,600
5.	Fixed overhead incurred		$39,300
6.	Production	18,000 units	
7.	Sales	17,500 units	$262,500
8.	Selling and administrative expenses		$32,400

Prepare an income statement for July showing all identifiable variances separately.

FINAL COMMENTS

1.   Process costing firms can use either actual costs or standard costs. Job order costing firms can use standard costs if they produce the same products over and over. Both types of firms can also use actual costs for labor and materials, while applying overhead based on units produced or direct labor hours worked.

2.   Under standard costing the flows of costs through work in process, finished goods, and cost of goods sold are at standard cost per unit multiplied by the number of units involved. For example, the account for cost of goods sold will show the standard cost of the number of units sold; finished goods inventory will show the standard cost of the number of units on hand.

CHAPTER 15

QUANTITATIVE METHODS AND MANAGERIAL ACCOUNTING

OVERVIEW

This chapter considers three quantitative techniques for solving various kinds of decision-making problems: statistical decision theory, inventory control methods, and linear programming.

Statistical decision theory was introduced in Chapter 5 in the context of using expected values in sales forecasting. The expected value approach can also be useful in determining whether or not to investigate cost variances and in selecting an appropriate strategy for firms that deal in perishable goods.

Inventory control is concerned with two basic decisions: when to place an order, and how much to order at a time. Each is discussed in some detail.

Linear programming is illustrated in a context of determining the optimal mix of products to produce when the firm is faced with two or more scarce resources (like available labor hours in different departments). The material on linear programming extends the analysis of Chapter 7, in which the problem of product selection under a single production constraint (fixed facility) is considered.

STATEMENTS FOR GUIDED READING

+   An optimal solution to a decision problem is one that provides the maximum expected profit.

+   The managerial accountant must be aware of various quantitative techniques even though he need not understand all of the mathematical analysis behind them.

+   Quantitative techniques rely on estimates about future conditions.

+   The expected value concept can be applied in situations in which there is uncertainty about future outcomes.

+   A variance from standard cost should be investigated if the expected benefits of investigation exceed the expected costs to investigate.

+   The value of perfect information is the maximum amount you would be willing to pay to eliminate uncertainty.

+   One convenient way to portray a decision problem is to use a decision tree.

+   Payoff tables, which show the expected values of actions, are useful in evaluating strategies under uncertainty.

+ The amount of inventory to be ordered at a particular time depends on the costs of carrying inventory and of placing the order to buy.

+ The reorder point is the level of inventory at which an order to replenish is placed.

+ The reorder point depends on the expected use of the product until the order is received and on the safety stock carried to reduce the possibility of running out.

+ Linear programming is a technique used in many decisions, for instance, what quantities of each product should be produced.

+ Linear programming frequently involves maximizing contribution margin where production is limited by two or more scarce resources.

+ The objective function in a linear programming problem is an equation that often represents the contribution margins of various products and the quantities of each to be produced.

+ After the manager has determined the optimal quantities of each product, he should perform some sensitivity analysis to see what would happen to the optimal solution if contribution margins were to change.

+ A shadow price is the value to be gained by relaxing a constraint, such as increasing the available hours of labor time or machine time in a particular department.

COMPREHENSION CHECK

<u>Directions</u>: Draw a line through the number of each false statement.

1. The use of sophisticated quantitative techniques requires estimates of future events.

2. A variance should be investigated if the amount of the variance is greater than the cost of investigation.

3. The reorder point is the level of inventory at which the firm places an order.

4. Safety stock is the level of inventory at which the firm places an order.

5. The EOQ model assumes that the use of inventory is constant throughout the year.

6. The salary of the purchasing agent is an example of an ordering cost that would be included in determining the EOQ.

7. If carrying costs increase, other factors remaining constant, the EOQ will decrease.

8. A major reason for carrying safety stock is to provide for potential fluctuations in use during the lead time.

9. If ordering costs increase, other factors remaining constant, the EOQ will decrease.

10. The costs associated with carrying inventory are more difficult to determine than the costs of stockouts.

11. Linear programming can be used only when the demand for each product is greater than the maximum amount of the product that the firm can produce.

12. A linear programming solution will nearly always provide for producing the maximum possible amount of the product with the highest contribution margin.

13. A firm that produces one product and has two or more scarce resources cannot benefit from the use of linear programming in setting output.

14. An optimal linear programming solution always occurs at an intersection of two lines.

15. The inequality $2X + 4Y \leqslant 600$ indicates that the firm can produce either 1,200 X or 2,400 Y.

16. A manager considering adding capacity in one of the firm's production departments should seriously consider the one with the lowest shadow price.

APPLICATIONS

Problem 1 Expected Values

The Cooper Company recently experienced an unfavorable variance. There is a 40% probability that it had a random cause and will not recur, a 60% probability that something is wrong with the process and that the variance in future periods will be $1,500. An investigation would cost $100 and if a problem is found, the probability of being able to correct it is 80%, with a 20% probability that it cannot be corrected.

Determine the expected costs of investigating and not investigating the variance.

Problem 2   Inventory Control

The Jamestown Furniture Company uses 6,000 bolts of cloth per year to make upholstery. Average annual carrying costs are $1.50 per bolt, and ordering costs are $180 per order. Safety stock is 500 bolts and the firm works 300 days per year. The lead time averages 8 days.

A.   Determine the reorder point.

B.   Determine the costs of ordering four, five, and six times per year.

Problem 3   Payoff Table

Roger Morgan operates the Fresh Lettuce Shop in a suburban shopping center. He buys head lettuce each morning for $.30 and prices them at $.50. He gives away unsold heads to an organization that provides meals for indigent citizens. Roger has estimated his daily demand for lettuce as follows:

Demand	Probability
500	20%
600	30%
700	30%
800	20%

Determine the optimal number of heads of lettuce that Roger should buy each day.

Problem 4   Linear Programming

The Manners Company makes two products, X and Y. Each requires time in two production departments, I and II. Data are given below.

	Product	
	X	Y
Contribution margin per unit	$5	$4
Time in department I, in hours	3	2
Time in department II, in hours	3	4

Department I has 84 hours of capacity available per week and department II 120 hours. All output can be sold. Use the graph below to plot the constraints and find the optimal output of each product.

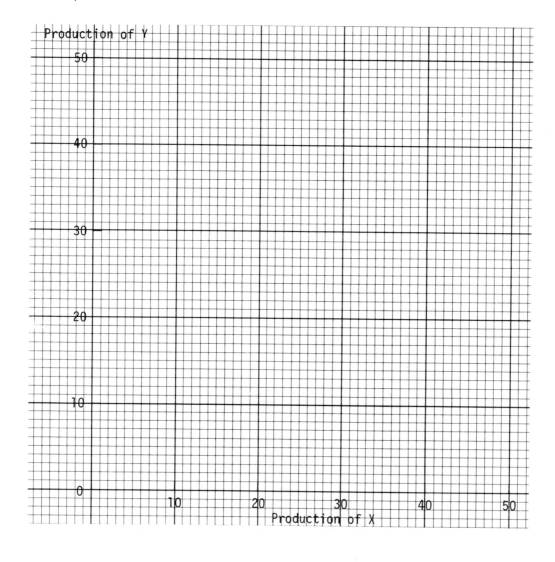

The president of the firm is wondering what would happen if the firm could increase capacity in department I to 90 hours per week. Plot the new constraint and find the new optimal solution and the value of the additional capacity.

CHAPTER 16

STATEMENT OF CHANGES IN FINANCIAL POSITION

OVERVIEW

Earlier chapters, especially Chapters 7-9, provided analytical tools to aid managers in their function as decision makers. The results of managers' decisions appear, sooner or later, in the firm's financial statements that are distributed outside the firm. Those who provide resources (through loans, stock investments, trade credit, etc.) to the firm want up-to-date knowledge of all of the firm's investing and financing activities, and are particularly interested in how managers balance the firm's available resources with needed resources. A formal statement of the firm's resource flows, the statement of changes in financial position, fills this information need.

Information about resource flows, if resources are defined as cash, is available to managers by reference to a firm's cash budget. A statement of changes in financial position, if resources are defined as cash, is merely a more formal presentation of the firm's cash budget.

For several reasons, managers and individuals outside the firm have found it useful to define resources not as cash but as working capital (current assets minus current liabilities). But the focus of interest remains the same: identifying from what sources a firm derives its resources and to what use those resources are put.

Because the statement of resource flows is a formal financial statement, its content and format are governed by Generally Accepted Accounting Principles. But the specific rules for such statements are few (three, to be exact) and relatively easy to understand. Probably the most difficult task in the preparation of a formal resource-flow statement arises because of an unwritten rule, the need to provide a reconciliation of net income, as shown on the formal income statement, with the amount reported as the resource inflow from operations. Development and understanding of such a reconciliation requires knowledge of the accrual basis of accounting.

As a formal financial statement, the statement of changes in financial position will be prepared by a firm's accounting staff and will be available to a firm's managers as well as to outside individuals. Nevertheless, managers should understand the concepts on which the statement is based and some of the problems in developing such a statement if they are to use it effectively. They should also understand how their actions affect the reported resource flows and how the reported flows will be interpreted by other readers.

QUESTIONS FOR GUIDED READING

+ Why are persons external to the firm interested in the flows of resources to and from the firm?

+ What are a firm's typical financing and investing activities?

+ Of the income statement and the statement of resource flows, which has the longer-term perspective?

+ In what ways do a formal statement of resource flows and a typical cash budget differ?

+ How are the income statement and a formal statement of resource flows related?

+ What are the other common names given to a formal statement of resource flows?

+ What alternatives are there for defining resources?

+ Why is it useful to define resources as working capital rather than as cash or cash and short-term investments?

+ What three basic rules govern the format and content of formal statements of changes in financial position?

+ What is the basic outline of a formal statement of changes in financial position?

+ Why does a typical statement of resource flows report transactions that did not affect resources as they are commonly defined?

+ Why is there a difference between net income and net cash inflow from operations?

+ Why is there a difference between sales and cash inflows from sales?

+ Why is there a difference between cost of goods sold and cash outflows for merchandise purchased?

+ Why is there a difference between operating expenses reported in the income statement and cash outflows for operating expenses?

+ If a cash budget is not available for study, is it possible to prepare a statement of changes in financial position using the cash concept of resources?

+ Why is there a difference between net income and working capital from operations?

+ What types of items that are required to reconcile net income and cash flow from operations are not required to reconcile net income and working capital from operations?

+ If a cash budget is not available for study, is it possible to prepare a statement of changes in financial position using the working capital concept of resources?

+ What is a schedule of working capital?

+ How do disposals of noncurrent assets complicate the preparation of a statement of changes in financial position?

+ What confusion has arisen because of the manner of reporting depreciation and similar costs in the statement of changes in financial position?

COMPREHENSION CHECK

<u>Directions:</u> Complete the following multiple-choice questions by placing the letter of the most appropriate answer available in the space provided.

_____ 1. A firm's financing activities:
  a. are of little interest to anyone except the firm's current top managers.
  b. are the resource inflows providing the means by which the firm can invest.
  c. include the purchase of other companies.
  d. show up most clearly in the firm's income statement.

_____ 2. The term resources:
  a. is generally understood to mean total assets.
  b. is a general term that can be defined in several ways.
  c. most often refers to stockholders' equity.
  d. means cash.

_____ 3. Working capital means:
  a. the excess of current assets over current liabilities.
  b. the amount of cash a firm has to cover day-to-day operations.
  c. the amount of money the firm has working for it in the form of inventory.
  d. the total of cash on hand plus short-term investments.

_____ 4. The working capital concept of resources is often used in the preparation of a statement of changes in financial position because:
  a. it incorporates information about the prospects of cash flows in the near future as well as about immediate flows.
  b. it is easier to understand than is the cash concept of resources.
  c. a firm usually wants to keep strictly confidential the details of its cash flows.
  d. many firms don't use cash budgets.

_____ 5. Which of the following is an alternative title for the statement of changes in financial position?
  a. balance sheet
  b. statement of changes in stockholders' equity
  c. schedule of working capital
  d. statement of funds flows

_____ 6. The major categories of a statement of resource flows might be identified as:
  a. funds used and funds applied.
  b. resource inflows and resources provided.
  c. funds provided and funds used.
  d. financing activities and investing activities.

_____ 7. Because it is universal practice to specifically report the firm's net income in its statement of changes in financial position:
  a. it is necessary to show a reconciliation of net income with funds provided by operations.
  b. some people confuse the funds statement with the income statement.
  c. there is no longer a need to provide an income statement as part of the package of formal financial statements.
  d. the working capital concept of resources has also received universal acceptance.

_____ 8. The cash budget of a firm:
    a. specifically shows the amount that will be reported by the firm as cash provided by operations.
    b. provides the information necessary for determining the amount to be reported by the firm as cash provided by operations.
    c. would be of little use in preparing a statement of changes in financial position based on the working capital concept of resources.
    d. is normally prepared in the format required for a statement of changes in financial position.

_____ 9. The reason net income does not coincide with cash provided by operations is:
    a. reported sales do not represent cash received this year from operating sources.
    b. reported cost of goods sold does not represent cash paid this year to merchandise suppliers.
    c. reported expenses do not represent cash payments this year for operating items.
    d. all of the above.

_____ 10. Which of the following would not be included in a reconciliation of net income with cash provided by operations?
    a. increase in accounts receivable
    b. decrease in land
    c. decrease in accounts payable
    d. depreciation expense for the year

_____ 11. Which of the following would not be considered a nonoperating ("other") use of cash?
    a. dividends paid to stockholders
    b. acquisition of buildings
    c. acquisition of inventory
    d. retirement of long-term debt

_____ 12. If a statement of changes in financial position were prepared using the working capital concept of resources:
    a. the reconciliation of net income to funds provided by operations is shorter than if the cash concept of resources were used.
    b. the reconciliation of net income to funds provided by operations would not include depreciation.
    c. the difference between funds provided and funds used would be equal to net income for the year.
    d. all financing and investing activities would automatically be included because all such activities affect working capital.

_____ 13. Which of the following items would appear in a reconciliation of net income and working capital provided by operations but would not appear in a reconciliation of net income and cash provided by operations?
    a. decrease in accrued liabilities
    b. amortization of bond discount
    c. increase in inventories
    d. None of the above is a good answer because all the listed items would appear in a reconciliation of net income to cash provided by operations.

_____ 14. A schedule of working capital:
   a. is a substitute for a statement of changes in financial position prepared using the working capital concept of resources.
   b. is a necessary adjunct to the statement of changes in financial position if the cash concept of resources is used for that statement.
   c. cannot be prepared until the net change in working capital is computed on the statement of changes in financial position.
   d. none of the above.

_____ 15. Which of the following would not appear in a reconciliation of net income and either cash or working capital provided by operations?
   a. proceeds from issuance of new long-term debt
   b. gain from sale of long-term investments
   c. depreciation expense for the year
   d. loss on the abandonment of obsolete equipment

APPLICATIONS

Problem 1

   Described below are thirteen transactions a company might engage in. To the right, below, are three columns headed with three possible concepts of resources: cash, working capital, and total assets. (Although the chapter did not specifically cover the idea of total assets as resources, that concept can be used as well as any of the others discussed. Its inclusion here is designed to help you develop facility in analyzing resource flows regardless of the definition of resources being used.)

   Read each transaction and then write, in the space provided in each column, the dollar effect such a transaction would have on resources defined as at the top of the column. As an example, consider a $10,000 cash sale of merchandise that had originally cost $6,000. Such a transaction would produce a $10,000 increase in (inflow of) resources if resources are defined as cash, a $4,000 increase ($10,000 cash in, less $6,000 of merchandise out) if resources are defined as working capital, and a $4,000 increase if resources are defined as total assets.

   If the listed transaction would have no effect on resources under one of the definitions, write NE in the appropriate blank.

	Resources Defined as		
Transactions	Cash	Working Capital	Total Assets
0. Sold, for $10,000 cash, merchandise that had originally cost $6,000	+10,000	+4,000	+4,000
1. Purchased merchandise for $8,000 on account			
2. Collected $5,000 cash on accounts receivable			
3. Borrowed $50,000 from the bank on a six-month note			
4. Wrote off a bad debt against the allowance for doubtful accounts			
5. Recorded the $2,500 estimated bad debts expense for the year			
6. Paid the $1,200 premium on a two-year insurance policy			
7. Recorded the $3,200 wages earned but not yet paid to employees			
8. Sold land that had cost $5,000, receiving $3,000 cash and a two-year note receivable for $7,000			
9. Recorded expiration of one-half of the insurance policy in transaction 6			
10. Issued 1,000 shares of $10 par stock for $13 per share cash			
11. Purchased a new machine, paying $3,000 in cash and giving a $7,000 three-year note for the balance			
12. Sold, for $1,800 cash, an old machine with a book value of $2,800			
13. Declared a dividend of $1,000 to be paid in cash in exactly one month			

Problem 2

All of the items listed below should appear in the 19X3 statement of changes in financial position for Thrill Company. Place each item in the appropriate place in the skeleton statement provided. The company follows the cash concept of resources.

Increase in merchandise inventory	$ 4,100
Decrease in accrued liabilities	2,300
Proceeds from sale of land	4,900
Proceeds from issuance of capital stock	28,600
Machinery acquired by giving a long-term note payable	18,800
Gain on sale of land	3,200
Decrease in accounts receivable	26,700
Decrease in accounts payable	15,800
Increase in prepaid expenses	700
Increase in income taxes payable	3,800
Net income	3,300
Dividends declared and paid	2,200
Increase in cash	2,600
Depreciation for the year	17,400
Purchase of new machinery	53,800

THRILL COMPANY
Statement of Changes in Financial Position
Cash Basis
for the Year 19X3

Resources provided by:
  Operations:

    Adjustments for items that affected net income
    but did not affect cash the same way:

    Total adjustments
    Cash provided by operations

  Cash provided by other sources:

        Total cash provided during the year
Resources used for:

        Total cash used during the year

Other financing and investing activities:

Problem 3

Using the same data as in Problem 2, prepare a statement of changes in financial position for the Thrill Company using the working capital concept of resources. Prove that the final number, the net change in working capital, is consistent with the information you have available regarding working capital.

FINAL COMMENTS

1.   At first, most students find it very difficult to prepare a reconciliation of net income and cash provided by operations. Usually, the problem is deciding whether to add or subtract the particular reconciling item, and the items that cause the most trouble are the changes in the various current asset and current liability accounts. Although memorizing rules will not aid in understanding what you are doing, the rules may serve you well until you have worked out the underlying logic for yourself. The only thing you have to know is whether a change in a particular item would increase working capital or decrease it. When you know in what direction working capital will be affected, you need only use the reconciling item in the opposite direction on the reconciliation. For example, an increase in accounts receivable would mean an increase in working capital; as a reconciling item, it would be a decrease adjustment.

2.   It is important to distinguish between changes in working capital and the reasons for changes in working capital. A statement of changes in financial position using the working capital concept of resources gives the reasons for or causes of working capital changes (operations, acquisitions of investments, distributions of dividends, etc.). An inventory increase, or cash decrease, or accounts payable increase is a change in working capital; it is not a reason for a change.

CHAPTER 17

ANALYZING FINANCIAL STATEMENTS

OVERVIEW

Although managers must concern themselves with day-to-day operations, they must always remember that the results of their decisions, insofar as those decisions affect the firm's financial statements, will ultimately be reviewed by individuals outside the entity. Such individuals include creditors, government officials, customers, employees, and investors. Hence, managers should know not only the analytical techniques that will help them in decision making, but also what techniques are used by outsiders (i.e., individuals external to the firm) to analyze the firm.

Analysis of a given firm may be very complex and involve studies of such things as the technological aspects of the product, the nature of competition in the industry, the experience of management personnel, and the general economic environment. But most financial observers agree that their analyses begin with the calculation and interpretation of various ratios that can be determined from typical published (or otherwise available) financial statements. For this reason, managers should become familiar with the most commonly used analytical ratios and the common interpretations of them. This chapter presents and discusses such ratios, emphasizing how management decisions can affect them and what limitations must be recognized when dealing with them.

QUESTIONS FOR GUIDED READING

+ What is the purpose of financial analysis?

+ In what respect are the perspectives or viewpoints of the analyst and the manager alike?

+ What are the three general areas or aspects about the firm with which analysts are normally concerned?

+ What is liquidity?

+ What sections of the financial statements are particularly relevant to the study of liquidity?

+ What is the working capital ratio and what is the biggest problem in trying to interpret that ratio?

+ What is the advantage of the quick ratio as a measure of liquidity?

+ What are the current asset activity ratios?

+ What factors besides the magnitudes of ratios must be considered in an evaluation of the liquidity of a particular company?

+   What is window dressing?

+   What ratios are used to assess a firm's profitability?

+   Why is there a difference between return on assets and return on equity?

+   What is leverage?

+   How does leverage affect a firm's profitability ratios?

+   What types of firms can safely use leverage?

+   Why is there a general interest in earnings per share?

+   What are the two variations in the computation of earnings per share and why are they necessary?

+   What are the two ratios dealing with a firm's dividends and how do they differ in computation and interpretation?

+   What is the price-earnings ratio and what is its significance?

+   What factors besides the magnitudes of ratios must be considered in an evaluation of the profitability of a particular company?

+   What is solvency?

+   What ratios or relationships are used to assess a firm's solvency?

+   How does leverage affect a firm's solvency ratios?

COMPREHENSION CHECK

Directions: Complete the following multiple-choice questions by placing the letter of the most appropriate answer available in the blank.

_____   1.   Which of the following is likely to employ financial analysts to help in making decisions about individual firms?
a.   mutual funds
b.   brokerage firms
c.   banks
d.   all of the above

_____   2.   The primary thrust of financial analysis is the:
a.   past.
b.   present.
c.   future.
d.   after-life.

_____   3.   Aspects of the firm important to the financial analyst's ratio analysis are:
a.   competition, management style, and product technology.
b.   liquidity, profitability, and solvency.
c.   the past, the present, and the future.
d.   working capital, income, and debt.

_____ 4. Which of the following ratios includes a component that is not part of the current sections of a balance sheet?
   a. working capital ratio
   b. inventory turnover
   c. quick ratio
   d. None of the above is a good answer because all of the listed ratios incorporate only items from the current sections

_____ 5. A major advantage of the quick ratio over the working capital ratio as a measure of liquidity is that the quick ratio:
   a. concentrates on current assets rather than current liabilities.
   b. is not affected by a firm's method of accounting for inventory.
   c. ignores accounting estimates such as the allowance for doubtful accounts.
   d. excludes marketable securities whose values fluctuate widely.

_____ 6. Which of the following ratios includes a component that is not from the balance sheet?
   a. acid-test ratio
   b. debt ratio
   c. accounts receivable turnover
   d. current ratio

_____ 7. Which of the following ratios includes a component that is not from the income statement?
   a. return on sales
   b. payout ratio
   c. times interest earned
   d. gross profit ratio

_____ 8. If a firm has 13 inventory turnovers per year, the approximate number of days' sales in its inventory is:
   a. 28.
   b. 13.
   c. 7.
   d. 365.

_____ 9. If a firm has a current ratio of 2.5 to 1 and just before the end of its fiscal year pays off a large short-term bank loan, its current ratio at the end of that year:
   a. will fall below 2 to 1.
   b. will be higher than it would have been had the loan been paid off just after the year's end.
   c. will be no different from what it would have been had the loan been paid off just after the year's end.
   d. will indicate that the firm has a liquidity problem.

_____ 10. A firm's return on assets will be lower than its return on equity as long as the firm:
   a. has any liabilities.
   b. has any long-term liabilities.
   c. continues to pay dividends.
   d. is successfully using leverage.

_____ 11. Leverage:
   a. relates to the manner in which a firm finances its assets.
   b. reduces the riskiness of an investment in the common stock of the leveraged firm.
   c. is particularly attractive for firms that operate in highly unstable industries.
   d. is a financing strategy designed to increase the dividends to holders of preferred stock.

_____ 12. The amount of earnings per share:
   a. is confidential information, release of which by a firm's management would bring action by government regulatory agencies.
   b. may have to be computed two different ways if a firm has outstanding some securities or obligations that represent potential for dilution of the firm's earnings.
   c. is likely to be very high for old established firms.
   d. is likely to be very high for firms that have high price-earnings ratios.

_____ 13. If a company has a high payout ratio:
   a. it is probably a growth company.
   b. it probably has a high price-earnings ratio.
   c. it may have had a particularly large drop in profit that year.
   d. it probably has few shares of stock outstanding.

_____ 14. Which of the following statements about solvency is true?
   a. A firm that is solvent would have no liquidity problems.
   b. A firm's solvency relates to the firm's debts and is of little concern to the firm's stockholders.
   c. A firm's solvency is of special concern to its long-term creditors.
   d. A firm's solvency is unrelated to the extent of its financial leverage.

_____ 15. Which of the following analytical ratios would not normally be classified as related to solvency?
   a. cash flow to total debt
   b. times interest earned
   c. debt ratio
   d. return on equity

_____ 16. Which of the following is true?
   a. Because it is desirable to be liquid, a firm should keep as much cash on hand as possible.
   b. Because leverage is advantageous to the stockholders, a firm should try to attain a high debt ratio.
   c. The current ratio of an electric utility would probably be lower than that of an automobile manufacturer.
   d. Just prior to the Christmas season, a department store would probably have higher than average current and quick asset ratios.

APPLICATIONS

Problem 1

Below are comparative financial statements for 19X7 and 19X6 for the UC Corporation, together with certain additional financial information. The data are only slight variations of data found in a current annual report of a multimillion dollar company operating in the United States.

UC Corporation
Comparative Balance Sheets
at December 31, 19X7 and 19X6

	19X7	19X6
ASSETS		
Current assets:		
Cash	$ 95	$ 115
Marketable securities	224	292
Accounts and notes receivable, net of allowances	1,090	1,038
Inventories	1,506	1,365
Prepaid expenses	147	100
Total current assets	3,062	2,910
Fixed assets:		
Machinery and equipment	7,231	6,586
Accumulated depreciation	3,690	3,460
	3,541	3,126
Land	300	250
Total fixed assets	3,841	3,376
Other assets	520	336
Total assets	$ 7,423	$ 6,622
EQUITIES		
Liabilities		
Current liabilities:		
Accounts payable	$ 377	$ 351
Debt due within one year	335	273
Taxes payable	219	186
Other accrued liabilities	487	436
Total current liabilities	1,418	1,246
Long-term debt	2,598	2,318
Total liabilities	4,016	3,564
Stockholders' equity		
Common stock	504	360
Retained earnings	2,903	2,698
Total stockholders' equity	3,407	3,058
Total equities	$ 7,423	$ 6,622

UC Corporation
Income Statements for the Years Ended
December 31, 19X7 and 19X6

	19X7	19X6
Sales	$ 7,484	$ 6,843
Cost of goods sold	4,681	4,317
Gross profit	2,803	2,526
Operating expenses:		
Depreciation	359	301
Selling and administrative	860	756
Research and development	170	150
Other	701	492
Total operating expenses	2,090	1,699
Income before interest and taxes	713	827
Interest expense	149	120
Income before taxes	564	707
Provision for income taxes	179	266
Net income	$ 385	$ 441

UC Corporation
Statement of Retained Earnings for the
Years Ended December 31, 19X7 and 19X6

	19X7	19X6
Balance, beginning of year	$ 2,698	$ 2,411
Net income	385	441
	3,083	2,852
Dividends ($2.80 per share in 19X7 and $2.50 per share in 19X6)	180	154
Balance, end of year	$ 2,903	$ 2,698

Additional financial information available to you is as follows:

1. All sales are on credit.

2. There is no preferred stock outstanding.

3. There are no securities or other obligations outstanding that offer potential dilution of common stock equity.

4. There were 65 shares of common stock outstanding throughout the year, and the price of one of those shares at the end of the year was $78.

    Based on all the financial information provided, compute the following items for the current year. Because the financial information was taken directly from the reports of an actual company, you cannot expect the ratios to "come out even." Carry your answers to one decimal place. (This would mean carrying your answers to three decimal places for percentages.)
    a. current ratio

    b. quick ratio

c. days' sales in accounts receivable

d. inventory turnover

e. return on assets

f. return on common equity

g. earnings per share (carry to 2 decimal places)

h. price-earnings ratio

i. gross profit ratio

j. return on sales

k. debt ratio

l. times interest earned

m. cash flow to debt

Problem 2 Effects of Transactions on Selected Ratios

Below are descriptions of transactions or events. To the right of each is a ratio that was computed immediately before the transaction described. Determine whether the transaction would increase (I) decrease (D), or have no effect on (N) the ratio listed, and place the appropriate letter in the space provided.

Effect	Transaction	Ratio
1. _____	Payment of cash on accounts payable	Current ratio of 3 to 1
2. _____	Purchase of merchandise for inventory, on account	Quick ratio of 2 to 1
3. _____	Annual recognition of bad debts expense, assuming that the firm uses an allowance account	Number of times bond interest is earned is 16.
4. _____	Annual recognition of depreciation on the company's building	Dividend yield of 8%
5. _____	Purchase of merchandise for inventory, on account	Gross profit ratio of 30%
6. _____	Purchase of merchandise on account	Number of inventory turnovers is 13.
7. _____	Sale of a machine at a price in excess of its book value	Earnings per share of $3.25
8. _____	Sale of a machine at a price lower than its book value	Current ratio of 4 to 1
9. _____	Write-off of an uncollectible account against the allowance for doubtful accounts	Quick ratio of 2 to 1
10. _____	Sale of merchandise, on account, for a price in excess of its cost	Return on assets of 18%
11. _____	Declaration of a cash dividend on common stock	Earnings per share of $3.50
12. _____	Collection of an account receivable	Quick ratio of 2 to 1

Problem 3 Working Backward

Below are the numerator and denominator that would be used in computing the common financial ratios indicated for an unnamed company.

Current ratio $= \dfrac{\$50,000}{\$15,000}$

Acid-test ratio $= \dfrac{\$36,000}{\$15,000}$

Inventory turnover $= \dfrac{\$180,000}{(\$10,000 + \$14,000)/2}$

Receivables turnovers $= \dfrac{\$250,000}{(\$28,000 + \$30,000)/2}$

Times interest earned $= \dfrac{\$10,000 + \$12,000 + \$8,000}{\$8,000}$

Earnings per share of common stock $= \dfrac{\$6,000}{15,000}$

Return on sales $= \dfrac{\$10,000}{\$250,000}$

Return on assets $= \dfrac{\$10,000 + \$8,000}{(\$285,000 + \$300,000)/2}$

Return on common stockholders' equity $= \dfrac{\$6,000}{(\$127,000 + \$130,000)/2}$

Dividend yield $= \dfrac{\$.20}{\$5.00}$

Additional known data are as follows:

1.   There are no prepaid expenses.

2.   Depreciation expense for the year was $28,000.

3.   All sales are on credit.

4.   The firm has $55,000 preferred stock issued and outstanding, and there were no changes during the year.

5.   There were no changes in the number of common shares outstanding during the year.

6.   The only change in total stockholders' equity were for income and dividends.

Based on all of the above information, fill in the blanks in the statements below.

a.   The current liabilities at the end of the year are $_____.

b.   The ending inventory was $_____.

c.   The gross profit for the year was $_____.

d.   The gross profit ratio for the year was _____%.

c.   The net purchases for the year were $_____.

f. The number of days' sales in the ending inventory is _____ days.

g. The income taxes for the year were $_____.

h. The market price of a share of the firm's common stock is $_____.

i. The firm's total liabilities at the end of the year were $_____.

j. The firm's long-term liabilities at the end of the year were $_____.

k. The firm's payout ratio is _____%.

l. The firm's ratio of cash flow to total debt is _____%.

m. The amount of preferred stock dividends was $_____.

FINAL COMMENTS

1. Ratio analysis is only the beginning in the total process of financial analysis. By its very nature as an analysis of what is (ratios are based on current or past performance or position), ratio analysis does not deal directly with what is of most interest to the analyst —the future. Hence, all conclusions reached on the basis of ratio analysis are at best tentative, and depend on the analyst's knowledge of expected changes for their applicability to the future.

2. As calculations based on past data, ratios are most useful when compared with their counterparts in prior years so that trends, if any, can be discerned. Although you must learn all the ratios that are commonly used, it is critical that you recognize that the absolute values of ratios are of no importance in themselves.

3.   Many students set out to memorize the multitude of ratio formulas in the chapter. In most cases, this effort is wasted because the statement of the name of the ratio tells you exactly how to compute it. For example, the current ratio quite obviously depends on the current sections of the balance sheet and "return" on sales could hardly be something other than income in relation to sales. Try to understand, in the simplest terms possible, what relationship each ratio states, and you will not have to memorize more than three formulas.

KEY

CHAPTER 1

COMPREHENSION CHECK

1. True   2. True

3. False: Management by objectives is associated with the planning function. Planning is the process of setting goals and developing methods to achieve them; management by objectives is setting objectives and trying to achieve them.

4. True   5. True

6. False: Line managers are responsible for the primary activities of the firm. Staff managers propose but cannot impose the recommendations they make to line managers; staff managers are advisers.

7. False: A pro forma statement is a forecast financial statement.

8. False: The managerial accountant is responsible for preparing reports that contain the information needed for the decision and should avoid a "kitchen sink" approach. The critical factor is the reporting of <u>relevant</u> information.

9. True   10. True

11. True

12. False: The selection of an appropriate measure of performance is an ongoing process which should be a constant concern of the managerial accountant.

13. True   14. True

15. False: The cost classification scheme for a managerial accounting report is usually by behavior of the cost or by responsibility for the cost. The question of <u>necessity</u> is one that cannot be answered by the managerial accountant.

16. True

17. False: Managerial accounting reports are concerned with the specific information requirements of managers and should be structured to serve these needs. There is no need for managerial accounting reports to conform to Generally Accepted Accounting Principles.

18. True

19. False: While the distinction between <u>need</u> and <u>want</u> may seem trivial at this point, it is an extremely important one. Few humans "want" to see information that indicates poor planning or inefficient performance.

20. True

APPLICATIONS

Problem 1

1.

A-1 Company
Income Statement
for January 1978

Sales		$10,000
Cost of sales		7,000
Gross margin		3,000
Operating expenses:		
Rent	$ 400	
Wages	1,500	
Depreciation	60	
Miscellaneous	140	2,100
Income before tax		900
Provision for income tax		180
Net income		$ 720

2.

A-1 Company
Balance Sheet
January 31, 1978

Current assets:		Current liabilities:	
Cash	$ 1,960	Accounts payable	$ 3,000
Inventory	4,000	Accrued income taxes payable	180
Total current assets	5,960	Total liabilities	3,180
Noncurrent assets:		Stockholders' equity	
Office furniture and equipment	8,000	Common stock, no par, 100	
Accumulated depreciation	2,060	shares authorized and issued	3,200
Total noncurrent assets	5,940	Retained earnings	5,520
		Total stockholders' equity	8,720
		Total liabilities and stock-	
Total assets	$11,900	holders' equity	$11,900

Problem 2

1.

A-2 Corporation
Income Statement
for the Year of 1978

Sales		$450,000
Cost of goods sold		310,000
Gross profit (or gross margin)		140,000
Operating expenses:		
Wages	$55,000	
Property tax	8,000	
Utilities	2,400	
Interest	10,500	
Insurance	400	
Office supplies	200	
Depreciation—building	4,000	
Depreciation—equipment	5,000	
Total operating expenses		85,500
Income before taxes		54,500
Income taxes		12,660
Net income		$ 41,840

2.

A-2 Corporation
Balance Sheet
December 31, 1978

ASSETS

Current assets:			
Cash		$ 40,300*	
Accounts receivable		60,000	
Inventory		90,000	
Total current assets			$190,300
Noncurrent assets:			
Land		35,000	
Building	$150,000		
Accumulated depreciation	13,800	136,200	
Equipment	70,000		
Accumulated depreciation	15,000	55,000	
Total noncurrent assets			226,200
Total assets			$416,500

EQUITIES

Current liabilities:			
Accounts payable			$ 60,000
Federal income taxes payable			2,660
Total current liabilities			62,660
Long-term liabilities:			
Bonds payable 8½% due 2001			100,000
Total liabilities			162,660
Stockholders' equity:			
Common stock, $2 par value, 100,000 shares			
authorized and outstanding		$200,000	
Retained earnings		53,840	253,840
Total liabilities and stockholders' equity			$416,500

*See T-account on the next page.

	Cash		
Beginning balance (12-31-77)	$ 4,000	$ 50,000	Notes payable
Cash sales	150,000	2,000	Interest
Collections on account	320,000	7,800	Property taxes
		8,000	Property taxes
		55,000	Wages
		8,500	Interest
		290,000	Accounts payable
		2,400	Utilities
		10,000	Federal income taxes
Ending balance (12-31-78)	$ 40,300		

CHAPTER 2

COMPREHENSION CHECK

1. c	4. c	7. c	10. c	13. a	16. a	19. c	22. d	25. b
2. b	5. a	8. b	11. c	14. d	17. b	20. b	23. b	26. d
3. a	6. d	9. a	12. b	15. c	18. d	21. d	24. b	27. d

APPLICATIONS

Abbreviations used below:

$$S = \text{Sales} \qquad\qquad CM = \text{Contribution margin}$$
$$VC = \text{Variable cost} \qquad I = \text{Income}$$
$$FC = \text{Fixed cost} \qquad\quad ROS = \text{Return on sales}$$

Problem 1

1. Sales price of \$6 less \$4 (\$2.50 + \$1.20 + \$.30) = \$2

2. $\qquad\qquad$ CM/sales price = \$2/\$6 = 33 1/3%

3. $\qquad\qquad$ FC/CM per unit = \$300/\$2 = 150 belts

4. $\qquad\qquad$ S = VC + FC, and VC = \$4/\$6 = 66 2/3%
   $\qquad\qquad$ S = 66 2/3% S + 300
   $\qquad$ 33 1/3% S = 300
   $\qquad\qquad$ S = \$900

   The answer can be arrived at more directly as FC/CM% = \$300/33 1/3% = \$900

5. 90 belts over break-even × \$2 CM = \$180 profit

6. $\qquad\qquad$
S	= \$4,800	(800 × \$6)
VC	= 3,200	(800 × \$4)
CM	= 1,600	
FC	= 300	
I	= \$1,300	

7. Start at the bottom of the income statement and work upwards.

S	$3,300	= (550 × $6)
VC	2,200	= (550 × 4)
CM	1,100	÷ CM of 2 per belt = <u>550 belts</u>
FC	300	
Profit required	<u>$ 800</u>	

8.

$$S = VC + FC + I$$
$$S = 66\ 2/3\%\ S + 300 + 20\%\ S$$
$$S = 86\ 2/3\%\ S + 300$$
$$13\ 1/3\%\ S = 300$$
$$S = \$2,250$$

or

$$S = FC/(CM\% - ROS\%)$$
$$S = 300/(.33\ 1/3 - .20)$$
$$S = 300/.13\ 1/3$$
$$S = \$2,250$$

9. Start at the bottom of the income statement and work upwards.

S	$3,900	($3,900/600 belts = $6,50)
VC	2,400	(600 × $4)
CM	1,500	($1,500/600 belts = $2.50 CM)
FC	300	
Profit desired	<u>$1,200</u>	

Problem 2

1.	Graph B	6.	Graph A
2.	Graph A	7.	Graph D
3.	Graph C	8.	Graph A
4.	Graph B	9.	Graph C
5.	Graph B		

Problem 3

AC	<u>Revenue line</u>	B	<u>Break-even point</u>
ED	<u>Total cost line</u>	G	<u>Break-even units</u>
DEF	<u>Variable costs</u>	H	<u>Break-even dollars</u>
CBD	<u>Profit area</u>	I	<u>Relevant range</u>
EBA	<u>Loss area</u>	EF	<u>Fixed cost line</u>

CHAPTER 3

COMPREHENSION CHECK

1. False: The sales dollars necessary to achieve a target after-tax profit would be under-
    stated if this computation were used. The calculation described would give an
    appropriate answer if the target profit were stated before taxes.

2. False: This type of agreement is representative of a mixed cost (semivariable cost); the
    set fee is a fixed cost, the percentage of sales dollars a variable cost.

3. True

4. False: If the fitted line hits the horizontal axis of the chart, the manager should prob-
    ably assume the chart has been plotted incorrectly since this would indicate total
    absence of cost at some positive level of volume. The fitted line should hit the
    vertical axis at the level of total fixed cost.

5. False: To assume that any single method should be used exclusively defines the task as
    well as the responsibility of the managerial accountant too narrowly. The mana-
    gerial accountant should use the method that provides the level of prediction
    accuracy sufficient for the problem at hand.

6. False: On the average, the middle line will come closest to predicting the actual cost.
    Important here is the concept that it is dangerous to categorize an unfavorable
    variance as "bad" or a favorable variance as "good" without understanding the
    underlying philosophy of planning employed.

7. False: Programmed costs and discretionary costs are synonymous. Discretionary costs and
    committed costs are complementary components of fixed costs.

8. False: Volume-cost-profit analysis assumes that managerial policies with regard to dis-
    cretionary costs to be incurred are stable.

9. True

10. False: Fixed costs may have both discretionary and committed elements. Additionally, a
    committed cost in one situation may be a discretionary cost in another situation.

11. False: As stated, the loss is less than the committed fixed costs. To halt the operation
    would ensure that the loss would equal the committed fixed costs.

12. False: And if you marked this freebie true, you are (1) dead, (2) distracted, or (3)
    totally indifferent.

13. False: Although employees who work directly on a firm's product are necessary, this cost
    is normally considered variable with the volume of production.

14. True   15. True

APPLICATIONS

Problem 1

a. Profit before taxes = X
    Taxes   = 20% of X
    Income   = 80% of X or $2,000

    If .8X = 2,000
        X = 2,500

    Therefore:
    Profit before taxes = $2,500   100%
    Taxes   =   500   20%
    Income   = $2,000   80%

b. Contribution margin = $14,500
    Fixed costs   = 12,000
    Profit before taxes =   2,500   100%
    Taxes   =   500   20%
    Income   = $ 2,000   80%

c. Sales per pair of boots   = $60
    Variable costs per pair of boots = 35
    Contribution margin per pair   = $25

    Total contribution margin needed $14,500

    $14,500 ÷ $25 = 580 pairs

Problem 2

a.

	High	Low	Change
Sales	$150,000	$30,000	$120,000
Repairs and maintenance	5,000	2,600	2,400

$$\frac{\text{Change in cost}}{\text{Change in sales}} = \frac{\$ 2,400}{\$120,000} = 2\%$$

b. High cost $5,000   Low cost $2,600
    2% of sales (.02 × 150,000)   3,000   2% of sales (.02 × 30,000)   600
    Fixed portion $2,000   Fixed portion $2,000

c.   Total cost = 2% of sales dollars + $2,000

d.

e. Variable cost = .02 × 132,000 $2,640
    Fixed cost   =   2,000
    Total cost $4,640

Problem 3

Sales	$22,000	
Variable costs	13,200	60% of sales dollars
Contribution margin	$ 8,800	
Fixed costs	5,000	
Profit before taxes	3,800	
Income taxes	1,140	30% of profit before taxes
Income	$ 2,660	

CHAPTER 4

COMPREHENSION CHECK

1. F	3. No match	5. R	7. No match	9. H	11. B	13. E
2. T	4. K	6. No match	8. J	10. C	12. Q	14. L

APPLICATIONS

Problem 1

The $600 positive or favorable difference between the planned and actual contribution margin is explained by the unfavorable sales price variance of $1,400 and the favorable sales volume variance of $2,000.

Difference in contribution margin ($5,000 - $5,600) = $600

Sales price variance	$1,400 unfavorable
Sales volume variance	2,000 favorable
Difference in contribution margin	$ 600

a.   Sales price variance = 1,400 units × ($15 - $14) = $1,400

b.   Sales volume variance = $5 × (1,000 units - 1,400 units) = $2,000

Problem 2

a. Method 1:

	A	B	C	Total
Planned sales	$1,000	$4,000	$5,000	$10,000
Variable costs	600	2,400	2,200	5,200
Contribution margin	$ 400	$1,600	$2,800	$ 4,800

$$\text{Total contribution margin} = \frac{\$ 4,800}{\$10,000} = 48\%$$

b.   Method 2:

	A	B	C	Total
Planned sales	$1,000	$4,000	$5,000	$10,000
Variable costs	600	2,400	2,200	
Contribution margin	$ 400	$1,600	$2,800	

1.   Contribution margin %

40%	40%	56%
($400/$1,000)	($1,600/$4,000)	($2,800/$5,000)

2.   Sales mix (percentage of total sales $)

10%	40%	50%
($1,000/$10,000)	($4,000/$10,000)	($5,000/$10,000)

3.   Contribution margin % × sales mix %

4%	16%	28%

4.   Total line 3 above to get the weighted average contribution margin.

48%

Problem 3

a.   Note that the sales mix is stated in units. For every 3 units sold, 2 of the units will be packages of hot dogs and 1 of the units will be a package of hot dog buns.

Sales batch:

	2 Packages of Hot Dogs	1 Package of Buns		Total for a Batch	
Sales	$2.40	$.60	=	$3.00	100%
Variable costs	1.80	.30	=	2.10	70%
Contribution margin	$ .60	.30	=	$ .90	30%
1. CM%	25%	50%			
2. Sales mix %	80%	20%			
3. Line 1 times line 2	20%	10%			

Weighted average
Contribution margin = 30%

b. $$\text{Break-even sales } \$ = \frac{\text{fixed cost}}{\text{CM\%}} = \frac{\$5,400}{.3} = \$18,000$$

c. $$\frac{\text{Total sales } \$ \text{ at break-even}}{\text{Sales } \$ \text{ per batch}} = \frac{\$18,000}{3} = 6,000 \text{ batches}$$

Each batch includes 2 packages of hot dogs and 1 package of hot dog buns, so sales at break-even equal 12,000 packages of hot dogs and 6,000 packages of hot dog buns.

Proof:

	Hot Dogs	Buns	Total
Sales	$14,400	$3,600	$18,000
Variable costs	10,800	1,800	12,600
CM	$ 3,600	$1,800	$ 5,400
FC			$ 5,400
Income			-0-

d.

$$\text{Sales dollars} = \frac{\text{FC + target profit before taxes}}{\text{weighted average CM\%}}$$

$$= \frac{5,400 + 12,000}{.3}$$

$$= \frac{17,400}{.3} = \$58,000$$

Problem 4

Discontinue Division B. The company will save $30,000 in fixed costs and will lose only $20,000 in contribution margin.

CHAPTER 5

COMPREHENSION CHECK

1.	a, b, c, e, f	5.	NONE	9.	a, d	13.	b, d
2.	b, c	6.	a	10.	d, e	14.	a, b, c, d, e
3.	b, d	7.	a, d	11.	a, b, c, d	15.	c, e
4.	c, d, e	8.	a, c	12.	a, e	16.	NONE

APPLICATIONS

Problem 1

 The probabilities add to 100%. Multiply each sales forecast by its assigned probability.

$$\$600,000 \times .1 = \$ 60,000$$
$$\$750,000 \times .5 = \$375,000$$
$$\$800,000 \times .35 = \$280,000$$
$$\$920,000 \times .05 = \$ 46,000$$

To get a single forecast add the computed numbers.

The expected value = $761,000

Problem 2

 The first step in solving this problem is to determine which of the items in the factory overhead are variable and which of the items are fixed. The variable items will vary in total amount as production varies and the fixed items will remain unchanged as production varies.

 Next, convert the variable items from a total amount into an amount per unit. Multiply the variable cost per unit by 1,200 units.

	Factory Overhead at 1,000 Units of Production	Likely Behavioral Pattern	Amount per Unit*	Factory Overhead at 1,200 Units of Production
Indirect labor	$1,500	variable	$1.50	$1,800
Supplies	750	variable	.75	900
Indirect material	500	variable	.50	600
Repairs	1,200	variable	1.20	1,440
Depreciation	1,000	fixed	⟶	1,000
Rent	600	fixed	⟶	600
Property taxes	300	fixed	⟶	300
Insurance	150	fixed	⟶	150
	$6,000			$6,790

*The per-unit amounts for costs identified as variable are forecast amounts (given in the problem) divided by forecast production of 1,000 units.

Variable factory overhead is $3.95 per unit ($1.50 + $.75 + $.50 + $1.20) and fixed factory overhead in total is $2,050 ($1,000 + $600 + $300 + $150). An all-purpose formula for factory overhead would be:

$$($3.95 \times production) + $2,050 = total factory overhead$$

Problem 3

	1,100 Units Revised Budget	1,100 Units Actual Costs	Variances
Material, variable $2 per unit	$ 2,200	$ 2,310	$110U
Labor, variable $4 per unit	4,400	4,290	(110)F
Indirect material, variable $.50 per unit	550	555	5U
Indirect labor, variable $1.00 per unit	1,100	1,050	(50)F
Repairs, variable $.70 per unit	770	760	(10)F
Depreciation, fixed	800	800	0
Property taxes, fixed	300	300	0
	$10,120	$10,065	($ 55)F

   Whether the cost of repairs is fixed or variable depends on the individual firm. It would be equally correct in this problem to consider repairs as a fixed cost.

Problem 4

Zero Company
Income Statement
for 1980

Sales (4,800 × $12)		$57,600
Cost of sales (4,800 × $7)		33,600
Gross profit		24,000
Variable selling expenses (4,800 × $1)		4,800
Contribution margin		19,200
Fixed salary	$12,000	
Rent	3,600	
Other fixed costs	1,800	17,400
Budgeted income		$ 1,800

CHAPTER 6

COMPREHENSION CHECK

1. True

2. False: Cash receipts for sales in any month are spread over a three-month period in the text example. In practice, the forecast of cash receipts should be based on past experience adjusted to any anticipated changes in conditions.

3. False: Although steady increases may be planned for and budgeted accordingly, unexpected increases might easily cause a cash <u>drain</u> that would place the firm in an extremely unfavorable cash position.

4. True   5. True

6. False: Inventory levels of goods available for sale would remain as planned, and the loan should have no effect on planned sales.

7. False: A lender would expect to see these statements in order to decide whether or not the firm is a worthwhile risk. In addition, top management would expect to receive forecast data.

8. True

9. False: The sales forecast, together with desired inventory policy, usually dictates the expected level of assets.

10. True

11. False: Only the best things in life are free; if you don't need cash, you're out of business. Moreover, it may be that the firm is inefficient in that its available funds exceed its anticipated demands for funds. Idle funds are not efficient.

12. True

13. False: Debt financing is more naturally related to fixed costs because of the fixed nature of interest commitments.

14. True   15. True

16. True   17. True

18. False: These procedures concentrate on individual items and the type of cost rather than on the objectives of the entity. Use of the most efficient means of accomplishing the objective may be precluded by strict adherence to the budget for a line item.

19. True

20. False: Zero-based budgeting is concerned with expenditures.

APPLICATIONS

Problem 1

A.
April Receipts

From April cash sales	($29,000 × 20%)	$ 5,800
From February credit sales	($22,000 × 80% × 60%)	10,560
From March credit sales	($25,000 × 80% × 40%)	8,000
Total cash from customers		$24,360

May Receipts

From May cash sales	($32,000 × 20%)	$ 6,400
From March credit sales	($25,000 × 80% × 60%)	12,000
From April credit sales	($29,000 × 80% × 40%)	9,280
Total cash from customers		$27,680

B. Accounts receivable, May 31, 19X0:

80% of May sales	($32,000 × 80%)	$25,600
60% of April credit sales	($29,000 × 80% × 60%)	13,920
		$39,520

Accounts receivable June 30, 19X0:

80% of June sales	($37,000 × 80%)	$29,600
60% of May credit sales	($32,000 × 80% × 60%)	15,360
		$44,960

Problem 2

A.
Budgeted Cash Disbursements, February 19X0

For accounts payable	$ 8,000 (January purchases)
For variable sales commissions	1,600 (1,600 × $1)
For fixed costs	2,500
	$12,100

Budgeted Cash Disbursements, March 19X0

For accounts payable	$ 8,600 (February purchases)
For variable sales commissions	1,720 (1,720 × $1)
For fixed costs	2,500
	$12,820

B.   Budgeted Income Statement for February 19X0

Sales	$16,000 (1,600 × $10)
Cost of sales	8,000 (1,600 × $5)
Gross profit	8,000
Variable selling expenses	1,600
Contribution margin	6,400
Fixed costs	3,100 ($2,500 + $600 depreciation)
Income	3,300
Income taxes	1,320
Net income	$ 1,980

C.   Budgeted Balance Sheet at
                                    February 28, 19X0

Assets		Equities	
Cash	$ 7,000	Accounts payable	$ 8,600
Accounts receivable	8,000	Taxes payable	2,480
Inventory	9,600		
Furniture and equipment	50,400	Common stock	40,000
Accumulated depreciation	(18,600)	Retained earnings	5,320
	$56,400		$56,400

Changes in Accounts

Cash:
Balance, January 31 balance sheet	$ 3,600
Collections on January sales	7,500
Collections on February sales	8,000
	19,100
February disbursements (part A)	12,100
	$ 7,000

Accounts Receivable:
Remaining balance of February sales ($16,000 × 50%)	$ 8,000

Inventory:
Balance, January 31 balance sheet	$ 9,000
February purchases given	8,600
	17,600
Cost of February sales (part B)	8,000
	$ 9,600

Accumulated Depreciation:
Balance, January 31 balance sheet	$18,000
February depreciation	600
	$18,600

Accounts Payable:
For February purchases	$ 8,600

Taxes Payable:
Balance, January 31 balance sheet	$ 1,160
February (part B)	1,320
	$ 2,480

Retained Earnings:
Balance, January 31 balance sheet	$ 3,340
February income (part B)	1,980
	$ 5,320

CHAPTER 7

<u>COMPREHENSION CHECK</u>

1. net income for the firm

2. expected future (or differential future)

3. sunk costs

4. opportunity cost

5. differential (incremental); opportunity

6. segments

7. unavoidable

8. joint

9. incremental loss

10. greater (larger)

11. complementary

12. negative

13. buy

14. joint process

15. split-off

16. sunk (irrelevant)

17. differential (incremental or marginal)

18. fixed facilities

19. discriminatory pricing

APPLICATIONS

Problem 1

A. Division D has a positive contribution margin and a positive segment margin of $23,000 ($43,000 - $20,000). In the short run, D should continue to operate.

B. and C. In the short run, the joint committed fixed costs of the company will remain. Consequently, if the remaining divisions (F and W) are allocated the $90,000 of joint committed fixed costs, the income of the firm would drop $23,000. If D is dropped, the income statement would be as below.

	F	W	Total
Sales	$109,600	$200,000	$309,600
Variable costs	54,000	80,000	134,000
Contribution margin	55,600	120,000	175,600
Separable fixed costs:			
Division manager's salary	(25,000)	(30,000)	(55,000)
Segment margin	30,600	90,000	120,600
Joint committed fixed costs, allocated equally	(45,000)	(45,000)	(90,000)
Income	($ 14,400)	$ 45,000	$ 30,600

Problem 2

Cost to Manufacture		Cost to Buy	
Variable costs:		Purchase Price	$30,000
Material	$20,000		
Labor	5,000		
Variable overhead	3,000		
	$28,000		$30,000

Zebra should continue to manufacture Z part unless $2,000 of fixed overhead costs can be eliminated. The current $4,000 of fixed overhead is irrelevant in the analysis and the decision because that cost would be incurred under either decision.

Problem 3

Sales price per pair		$20 per pair
Variable costs per pair		$15 per pair
Contribution margin per pair	($20 - $15) × 3,000 pairs	$15,000

Income would have increased by $15,000.

Recognizing that fixed costs would not be affected by the new order, the total contribution margin on the order would have increased the firm's profit. Hence, the profit foregone by rejection of the order was $15,000.

Problem 4

A. $5.00

Sales price		$30.00
Variable costs:		
Material	$ 4.00	
Labor	16.00	
Overhead	2.00	
Manufacturing costs	$22.00	
Selling	3.00	
Total variable costs		25.00
Contribution margin		$ 5.00

B. $2.50   ($5/2 hrs.)

C. Sales price $10.00
   Variable costs:
     Material $1.50
     Labor   4.00
     Overhead   .50
       Manufacturing costs   6.00
     Selling   1.00
     Total variable costs   7.00
   Contribution margin $ 3.00

D. $6.00   ($3/.5 hrs.)

E. $1,100

   Fixed manufacturing   ($1 × 600) $ 600
   Fixed selling and administrative $26,000/52   500
   Total fixed costs $1,100

F. If only T were produced, the weekly income statement would appear as follows:

   Sales   (300 at $30) $9,000
   Variable costs:
     Manufacturing   (300 at $22) $6,600
     Selling   (300 at $3)   900   7,500
   Contribution margin   1,500
   Fixed costs:
     Manufacturing   600
     Selling and administrative   ($26,000/52)   500   1,100
   Income $ 400

G. If only G were produced, the weekly income statement would appear as follows:

   Sales   (1,200 at $10) $12,000
   Variable costs:
     Manufacturing   (1,200 at $6) $7,200
     Selling   ($1 × 1,200)   1,200   8,400
   Contribution margin   3,600
   Fixed costs:
     Manufacturing   ($1 × 600)   600
     Selling and administrative   500   1,100
   Income $ 2,500

H. The firm should concentrate on the production and sale of G's.

Problem 5

A. Analysis of whether or not to produce after split-off:

Products	Incremental Revenue	Incremental Cost	Conclusion
A	$6,000 ($12,000 - $6,000)	$3,000	Produce after split-off
B	1,000 ($10,000 - $9,000)	2,000	Sell at split-off
C	2,500 ($2,500 - $0)	1,000	Produce after split-off

B. Product line income statements:

	Products			
	A	B	C	Total
Sales	$12,000	$9,000	$2,500	$23,500
Costs:				
Joint costs	(2,000)	(3,000)	---	(5,000)
Additional processing costs	(3,000)	-0-	(1,000)	(4,000)
Income	$ 7,000	$6,000	$1,500	$14,500

COMPREHENSION CHECK

1. B	4. No answer	6. M	8. G	10. H	12. O
2. C	5. K	7. E	9. No answer	11. N	13. L
3. I					

APPLICATIONS

Problem 1

A.

Tax Computation		Cash Flow
Revenue	$72,000	$72,000
Depreciation	40,000	
Taxable income	32,000	
Tax 25%	8,000	(8,000)
Income	$24,000	
Annual net cash flow		$64,000

B.   Payback = $120,000 divided by $64,000 = 1.875 years or 1 year, 10½ months

C.   Present value of future net cash flows equals:

$$\begin{array}{lr} \$64,000 \times 1.981 = & \$126,784 \\ \text{Cost of the machine} & 120,000 \\ \text{Net present value} & \$\;\;6,784 \end{array}$$

D.   1.   Annual net income $24,000 (part 2)

    2.   Average book value of machine $60,000 ($120,000/2)

    3.   Average book rate of return 40% ($24,000/$60,000)

E.   If net cash flows drop to $60,000:

$$\begin{array}{lr} \text{PV of future net cash flows } \$60,000 \times 1.981 & \$118,860 \\ \text{Cost of machine} & 120,000 \\ \text{Net present value} & (\$\;\;1,140) \end{array}$$

The NPV is negative; therefore, the machine is not earning the desired rate of return. Note that the machine needs to have an annual net cash flow of $60,576 in order to earn the desired rate of return.

1.981 times annual net cash flow	120,000
Cost of machine	120,000
Net present value	-0-

$$1.981 \text{ times NCF} = 120,000$$
$$\text{NCF} = 120,000 \times 1.981$$
$$\text{NCF} = \$60,575.466$$

Problem 2

A.

Annual cash savings	$9,600
Depreciation	3,200 [($34,000 - $2,000)/10]
Income before taxes	6,400
Taxes (25%)	1,600
Net income	4,800
Add back depreciation	3,200
Net cash flow	$8,000

B. Payback = $34,000/$8,000 = $4\frac{1}{4}$ years.

C.

PV of annuity of $8,000 per year for 10 years, when I = 20%	
8,000 × 4.192	$33,536
PV of salvage $2,000 × .162	324
Present value of future net cash flows	33,860
Cost of investment	34,000
Net present value	($ 140)

D. The net present value is negative. The machine should not be purchased.

E. An estimate of the internal rate of return is $19\frac{1}{2}$%. When the cash flows were discounted at 20% the negative net present value was small; therefore, the investment is earning almost 20%.

This answer can also be estimated by tracing the payback period to the table for the present value of an annuity. The payback factor (4.25) is between the factors for 18% (4.494) and 20% (4.192). Of course, this approach does not give consideration to the return provided by the salvage value. You could, however, test this answer by reference to, as stated first, the relatively small negative net present value computed in part C when the 20% rate was used.

Problem 3

A.

	Year 1	Year 2	Year 3
Cash revenues less cash operating costs	$96,000	$54,000	$37,000
Less depreciation*	55,000	36,667	18,333
Income before taxes	41,000	17,333	18,667
Taxes (50%)	20,500	8,667	9,334
Net income	20,500	8,666	9,333
Add back depreciation	55,000	36,667	18,333
Cash provided from sale of machine			50,000
Net cash flow	$75,500	$45,333	$77,666

*Depreciable cost of $110,000 ($160,000 - $50,000) allocated 3/6, 2/6, and 1/6.

B.
PV of net cash flow at end of year 1	$ 68,630 ($75,500 × .909)
PV of net cash flow at end of year 2	$ 37,445 ($45,333 × .826)
PV of net cash flow at end of year 3	$ 58,327 ($77,666 × .751)

Total	$164,402
Cost of investment	160,000
Net present value	$ 4,402

C. Yes; the net present value was positive.

D. Payback:

Cash flow received during first year = $75,500
Cash flow needed to get back remainder of investment = $120,000 - $75,500
= $44,500

The payback computation assumes cash flows are spread evenly throughout the year. So the company needs $44,500 of $45,333 or 98% of the second year's net cash flow. Payback is 1.98 years.

Problem 4

Acquisition of the new oven would seem to be a wise decision.

	Tax	Cash
New cash operating costs	($1,500)	($ 1,500)
Savings on variable cost of using new bun machine		
$.04 × 200,000	8,000	8,000
Depreciation on new bun machine $8,000/4	(2,000)	
Net savings, before taxes during coming years	4,500	
Tax on the cost savings (40%)	1,800	(1,800)
Net annual cash savings from buying and operating the bun machine		$ 4,700
Present value of future operating savings		
(factor for 4 yrs. at 10%)		3.170
Present value of future operating savings		14,899
Cost of purchasing the new bun machine		
(automatically equal to present value)		8,000
Net present value of acquiring the new bun machine		$ 6,899

CHAPTER 9

COMPREHENSION CHECK

1.	c	4.	b	6.	c	8.	d	10.	c	12.	a
2.	c	5.	b	7.	a	9.	d	11.	d	13.	c
3.	b										

APPLICATIONS

Problem 1

A.   Total project approach

   1.   Keep old equipment

			Cash Flow Years 1, 2, & 3	Cash Flow Year 4
Tax Computation				
Depreciation	$10,000			
Operating costs	10,000	($2,000 + $8,000)	($10,000)	($10,000)
Total costs	20,000			
Tax shield (40%)	8,000		8,000	8,000
Net cash flow for years 1, 2, & 3			($ 2,000)	
Selling price of equipment, cash, no gain or loss on sale				5,000
Net cash flow, year 4				$ 3,000
PV of cash flows for years 1, 2, & 3 ($2,000) × 2.174				($ 4,348)
PV of cash flow for year 4 $3,000 × .516				1,548
Present value of cash flows, net outflow				($ 2,800)

   2.   Buy new machine

Tax Computation				
Depreciation	$17,500	($70,000/4)		
Operating costs	2,000		($ 2,000)	($ 2,000)
Total costs	19,500			
Tax shield (40%)	7,800		7,800	7,800
Net cash flow			$ 5,800	
Cash from return of working capital investment				10,000
Net cash flow				$15,800

Net cost of investment at beginning of year 1

	Tax Computation	Cash Flow
Purchase cost		($70,000)
Additional investment in working capital		(10,000)
Sales price of equipment	$60,000	
Book value of equipment sold	45,000	
Gain on sale	15,000	
Tax on gain (40%)	6,000	(6,000)
Net cost of investment, outflow		($26,000)
PV of cash flows years 1, 2, and 3		
$5,800 × 2.174		$12,609
PV of cash flow year 4		
$15,800 × .516		8,153
PV of future cash flows		20,762
Net cost of investment		(26,000)
Net value of cash flows		($5,238)

3. Comparison of alternatives

Keep old equipment—PV of cash flows	($2,800)
Buy new machine—PV of cash flows	(5,238)
Better off keeping old equipment by	$2,438

B. Incremental approach

Considering only the items that would change if the new machine were purchased.

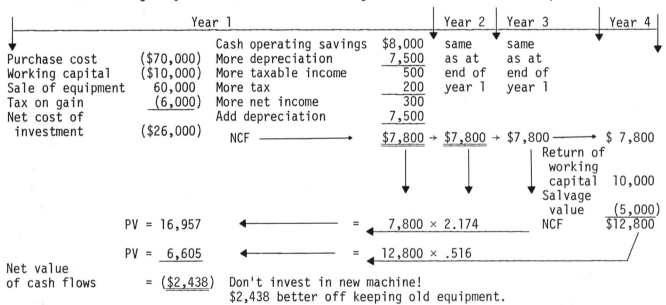

Net value of cash flows = ($2,438) Don't invest in new machine!
$2,438 better off keeping old equipment.

Note that the total project approach and the incremental approach give you the same answer.

Problem 2

A.   Alternative 1—Buy Mercedes

Present value of cash flows associated with buying the Mercedes:

	Tax Computation	Cash Flow	Present Value
Annual operating costs	$1,100	($ 1,100)	
Depreciation (12,000/6)	2,000		
Total costs	3,100		
Tax savings (60%)	1,860	1,860	
Net cash flow		760	
PV factor for 6-year annuity at 12%		4.111	$ 3,124
Salvage value		3,000	
PV of $1 when N = 6, I = 12%		.507	1,521
Purchase price			(15,000)
Present value of future flows			($10,355)

B.   Alternative 2—Buy Sedans

Present value of cash flows associated with buying the sedans:

	Tax Computation	Cash Flow	Present Value
Annual operating costs	$ 900	($ 900)	
Depreciation (6,000/3)	2,000		
Total costs	2,900		
Tax savings	1,740	1,740	
Net cash flow		840	
PV factor for 6-year annuity at 12%		4.111	$ 3,453
Salvage value at end of year 3		$ 2,000	
Cost of second sedan		(8,000)	
Net cost		(6,000)	
PV of $1 when N = 3, I = 12%		.712	(4,272)
Salvage value at end of year 6		$ 2,000	
PV of $1 when N = 6, I = 12%		.507	1,014
Purchase price of first sedan			(8,000)
Present value of future cash flows			($ 7,805)

C.   The computations indicate that the firm should buy sedans; the present value of the cash outflows associated with that alternative is lower.

CHAPTER 10

COMPREHENSION CHECK

1. d	3. a	5. c	7. d	9. a	11. b	13. d
2. b	4. c	6. a	8. d	10. b	12. b	14. b

APPLICATIONS

Problem 1

A. Total hours of use equal 2,500.

Lee Division	(1,000/2,500) × $92,450	$36,980
Grant Division	(1,500/2,500) × $92,450	55,470

Note that under this method, all of the actual costs are allocated to using departments.

B.
Lee Division	$36,000
Grant Division	54,000
Total allocated costs	$90,000
Unallocated costs	$ 2,450

C. Lee Division:
Fixed costs of (1,200/2,600) × $60,000	$27,692
Variable costs of $12 × 1,000 hours	12,000
	$39,692

Grant Division:
Fixed costs of (1,400/2,600) × $60,000	$32,308
Variable costs of $12 × 1,500 hours	18,000
	$50,308

Allocated costs	($39,692 + $50,308)	$90,000
Unallocated costs	($92,450 - $90,000)	$ 2,450

Problem 2

A. $230. This is the selling price for Center A, all of whose output goes to Center B.

B. A variable cost to Center B. The total cost will vary directly with the number of units required.

C.

Center A
Income Statement
for One Year

Sales	(1,000 × $230)	$230,000
Variable cost	(1,000 × $90)	90,000
Contribution margin		140,000
Fixed costs		120,000
Income		$ 20,000

Center B
Income Statement
for One year

Sales	(1,000 × $600)	$600,000
Variable cost	[1,000 × ($230 + $300)]	530,000
Contribution margin		70,000
Fixed cost		10,000
Income		$ 60,000

Heather Corp.
Income Statement
for One Year

Sales	$600,000	
Variable cost	390,000	[1,000 × ($90 + $300)]
Contribution margin	210,000	
Fixed cost	130,000	($120,000 + $10,000)
Income	$ 80,000	

CHAPTER 11

COMPREHENSION CHECK

1. decentralized

2. exception

3. controllable

4. profits

5. return on investment

6. income

7. investment turnover

8. rate of return

9. investment

10. return on investment

11. liabilities

12. original cost less accumulated depreciation

13. amortizing

14. market prices

APPLICATIONS

Problem 1

1. Return on investment (ROI) = $10,000 ÷ $80,000 = 12½%

2. Minimum desired ROI = $80,000 × 10% or $8,000

3. Residual income = $10,000 - $8,000 = $2,000

4. Return on sales = $10,000 ÷ $48,000 = 20.8%

5. Investment turnover = $48,000 ÷ $80,000 = .6 times

6. a.

Incremental revenue	$24,000 (1,500 × $16)
Incremental variable costs	15,000 (1,500 × $10)
Incremental contribution margin	9,000
Incremental fixed costs	6,000
Incremental divisional profit	$ 3,000

    b.

Divisional profit = $10,000 + 3,000	$13,000
10% of investment = 10% of $120,000	12,000
Residual income	$ 1,000

    c. No. Residual income will decline by $1,000 ($2,000 - $1,000).

Problem 2

Project	Required Investment	Expected Income	Required Return of 14%	Residual Income	New Investment	Expected Income
Alpha	$100,000	$14,000	$14,000	$ -		
Beta	50,000	8,000	7,000	1,000	$ 50,000	$ 8,000
Sigma	23,000	4,000	3,220	780	23,000	4,000
Omega	17,000	1,530	2,380	(850)		
Phi	33,400	4,000	4,676	(676)		
Psi	72,000	14,400	10,080	4,320	72,000	14,400
Pi	38,000	6,080	5,320	760	38,000	6,080
Delta	14,500	2,000	2,030	(30)		
Chi	6,800	800	952	(152)		
New investment					183,000	32,480
Current investment and income					450,000	103,500
Total					$633,000	$135,980
Minimum return required	14% × $633,000					88,620
Expected residual income						47,360
Current residual income	$103,500 - (14% × $450,000)					40,500
Expected increase in residual income						$ 6,860

The firm may or may not choose to undertake project Alpha, which promises a return exactly equal to the required return.

Problem 3

	Case I	Case II	Case III
Sales	$100,000	$40,000	$225,000
Income	$ 6,000	$ 4,000	$ 9,000
Investment turnover	2 times	2 times	2.25 times
Return on sales	6 %	10%	4%
Return on investment	12%	20%	9%
Investment	$ 50,000	$20,000	$100,000
Residual income	$ 1,000	$ 2,000	$ (1,000)

Problem 4

A. Partial income statements for three divisions:

	Divisions		
	Mini	Micro	Maxi
Sales 500 @ $40	$20,000		
1,500 @ $15		$22,500	
500 @ $150			$75,000
Variable costs:			
500 minis @ $40			(20,000)
1,500 micros @ $15			(22,500)
VC—Maxi Division			
$42 per unit			(21,000)
VC—Mini Division			
$20 per unit	(10,000)		
VC—Micro Division			
$9 per unit		(13,500)	
Contribution margin	$10,000	$ 9,000	$11,500

B. Partial income statement for Master Corporation as a whole. All intracompany transfers have been eliminated:

Sales			$75,000
Variable costs:	Mini	$10,000	
	Micro	13,500	
	Maxi	21,000	44,500
Contribution margin			$30,500

CHAPTER 12

COMPREHENSION CHECK

1. d	3. a	5. b	7. c	9. d	11. d	13. a
2. c	4. c	6. a	8. a	10. b	12. a	14. a

APPLICATIONS

Problem 1

Material:		
Quik	3½ yds. at $2.80	$ 9.80
Wink	9 yds. at $1.10	9.90
Labor:		
Smoothing	1½ hrs. at $6.50	9.75
Packing	1 hr. at $4.00	4.00
Variable overhead	2½ hrs. at $7	17.50
Total		$50.95

Problem 2

A. 1. 25,000 units × 6 lbs. per unit × $1 per lb. $150,000

    2. 25,000 units × .5 gals. per unit × $4.80 per gal.   60,000

    3. 25,000 units × .5 hrs. per unit × $7.20 per hr.   90,000

    4. 25,000 units × .5 hrs. per unit × $10 per hr.   125,000

B. 1.
Actual material purchases 142,500 × $1.04		$148,200
Standard cost of purchasing the materials		
142,500 × $1		142,500
Material price variance, unfavorable		$ 5,700

Or, using the alternative method:

Actual price of material	$ 1.04 per lb.
Standard price of material	1.00 per lb.
Excess price	$ .04 per lb.
Quantity of material purchased	142,500 lbs.
Material price variance, unfavorable	$ 5,700

2. Actual material purchases   14,200 × $4.75 $67,450
    Standard cost of purchasing the materials
      14,200 × $4.80   68,160
    Material price variance, favorable $ 710

    Or, using the alternative method:

    Actual price of material $ 4.75 per gal.
    Standard price of material   4.80 per gal.
    Savings   .05 per gal.
    Quantity of material purchased   14,200 gals.
    Material price variance, favorable $ 710

3. Standard cost of material used
      142,500 × $1 $142,500
    Standard cost of quantity of material that
      <u>should</u> have been used (the flexible budget
      allowance at the output achieved)
      23,800 units × 6 lbs. per unit × $1   142,800
    Material use variance, favorable $ 300

    Or, using the alternative method:

    Quantity of material used   142,500 lbs.
    Quantity of material that should have been used
      23,800 × 6 lbs.   142,800 lbs.
    Savings in materials   300 lbs.
    Standard cost of material $1 per lb.
    Material use variance, favorable $300

4. Standard cost of material used
      (14,200 - 2,200) × $4.80 $57,600
    Standard cost of quantity of material that
      <u>should</u> have been used (the flexible budget
      allowance at the output achieved)
      23,800 units × .5 gals. per unit × $4.80   57,120
    Material use variance, unfavorable $ 480

    Or, using the alternative method:

    Quantity of material used   14,200 - 2,200   12,000 gals.
    Quantity of material that should have been
      used   23,800 × .5   11,900 gals.
    Excess gallons used   100 gals.
    Standard cost per gallon $4.80
    Material use variance, unfavorable $480

5. Actual labor cost   11,700 hrs. × $7.15 per hr. $83,655
    Standard cost of quantity of labor used
      11,700 hrs. × $7.20 per hr.   84,240
    Labor rate variance, favorable $ 585

Or, using the alternative method:

Actual cost per labor hour	$7.15
Standard cost per hour	7.20
Savings	$ .05
Quantity of hours purchased	11,700
Labor rate variance, favorable	$ 585

6. Standard cost of labor used   11,700 × $7.20 $84,240
   Standard cost of labor that should have been
   used (the flexible budget allowance at the
   output achieved)   23,800 × .5 × $7.20   85,680
   Labor efficiency variance, favorable $ 1,440

   Or, using the alternative method:

Quantity of hours used	11,700 hrs.
Quantity of hours that should have been used 23,800 × .5	11,900 hrs.
Hours under standard	200 hrs.
Standard cost per hour	$7.20
Labor efficiency variance, favorable	$1,440

7. Actual overhead for the year $119,300
   Standard cost of overhead for the quantity
   of labor hours used   11,700 × $10   117,000
   Spending variance, unfavorable $ 2,300

8. Standard cost of overhead for the quantity of
   labor hours used   11,700 × $10 $117,000
   Standard cost of overhead for the quantity of
   overhead that should have been incurred based
   on production achieved (flexible budget
   allowance based on output)   23,800 × $5   119,000
   Variable overhead efficiency variance, favorable $ 2,000

Note that this variance can be checked by reference to the labor efficiency variance. As in part 6, labor use was 200 hours under standard. The variable overhead efficiency variance should be (and is) the savings in labor hours (200) times the variable overhead cost per hour ($10).

CHAPTER 13

COMPREHENSION CHECK

1. False: Absorption costing inventory includes fixed costs, while variable costing inventory does not. Therefore, absorption costing inventory will be higher than variable costing inventory, per unit and in total.

2. True

3. False: Variable selling and administrative costs are not included in inventory.

4. True   5. True

6. True   7. True

8. False: Income will be affected by production under <u>any</u> absorption costing method. Whether unit costs incorporate actual or standard fixed costs, the result is still some form of absorption costing.

9. False: The volume variances arise because production is different from the denominator used to determine the standard fixed cost per unit. A "favorable" volume variance means only that actual volume exceeded that volume level used to compute the standard cost.

10. True

11. False: Both methods treat variable selling and administrative costs as expenses in the period incurred.

12. False: The volume variance relates to production, not sales.

13. True   14. True

15. True   16. True

17. True

18. False: Standard per-unit fixed costs are used for product costing, but not for planning and control. Cost predictions precede the computation of standard per-unit fixed costs.

19. False: The selection of the level to be used in setting a standard fixed cost per unit is a matter of managerial preference and has no "real" effects on the firm.

20. False: Absorption costing does not consider selling and administrative costs in determining product cost; moreover, for firms that face competition, prices are determined by market forces, not by managerial judgment.

APPLICATIONS

Problem 1

Miller Company
Income Statement for 19X8

		Variable Costing
Sales (80,000 × $20)		$1,600,000
Cost of goods sold (80,000 × $8)		640,000
Gross profit		960,000
Variable selling and administrative expenses		80,000
Contribution margin		880,000
Fixed costs:		
Production	$240,000	
Selling and administrative	300,000	540,000
Income		$ 340,000

		Absorption Costing
Sales		$1,600,000
Cost of goods sold:		
Beginning inventory	$ 0	
Variable production costs	800,000	
Fixed production costs	240,000	
Total	1,040,000	
Less ending inventory (20,000 × $10.40)*	208,000	832,000
Gross profit		768,000
Selling and administrative expenses		380,000
Income		$ 388,000

*$1,040,000/100,000 = $10.40 per unit

Problem 2

A.   Predetermined overhead rate = $2 per direct labor hour ($100,000/50,000)

	Standard Fixed Costs	
	X	Y
Direct labor hours required	.5	1.0
Predetermined overhead rate	$2	$2
Standard fixed cost per unit	$1.00	$2.00

B.

Ralston Company
Income Statement for 19X8

Sales (35,000 × \$10) + (25,000 × \$20)		\$850,000
Standard cost of sales [(35,000 × \$4) + (25,000 × \$14)]*		490,000
Standard gross profit		360,000
Budget variance (\$100,000 - \$98,500)	\$ 1,500F	
Volume variance†	10,000U	8,500
Actual gross profit		351,500
Selling and administrative expenses		220,000
Income		\$131,500

	X	Y
*Standard cost:		
Variable production cost	\$ 3	\$12
Fixed production cost (part A)	1	2
	\$ 4	\$14

†Applied fixed overhead was \$90,000 [(40,000 × \$1) + (25,000 × \$2)], which is \$10,000 less than budgeted fixed overhead of \$100,000.

CHAPTER 14

COMPREHENSION CHECK

1. False: Equivalent production will be the same for both firms.

2. False: General Motors produces a number of models, but all must undergo almost the same processes so that it most likely uses standard costs.

3. False: Variances could be either favorable or unfavorable in total so that the standard costing firm could show either higher or lower incomes than the actual costing firm.

4. True

5. False: FIFO can be used for control purposes because it involves computing unit costs using only the current period's production costs. The weighted average method combines costs and production for the current and prior period to arrive at a single unit cost.

6. True   7. True

8. True

9. False: It is isolated at the time of purchase of materials. The use variance is identified with the use of materials.

10. False: If it makes the same basic products over and over again, it can use standard costs.

11. False: If a job order firm uses a predetermined overhead rate (which is very likely), it will show a volume variance if overhead absorbed is different from budgeted overhead.

12. False: When there are semifinished units on hand in a firm that uses process costing, equivalent production must be calculated so that a cost can be assigned to the in-process inventory.

13. True

14. False: A job order firm will most likely use a predetermined overhead rate for applying overhead. It may be a relatively simple task to identify the actual materials and labor costs for a particular job; it would be impossible to identify the actual overhead applicable to a particular job.

15. True   16. True

17. True

APPLICATIONS

Problem 1

A.

	M-1	M-2
Materials	$ 65,000	$ 74,000
Direct labor	210,000	180,000
Overhead at $1.50 per direct labor dollar*	315,000	270,000
Total costs	$590,000	$524,000

*$7.50/$5.00

B.

York Vault Company
Income Statement for March 19X6

Sales		$810,000
Cost of goods sold		590,000
Gross profit		220,000
Underapplied overhead*	$15,000	
Selling and administrative expenses	87,000	102,000
Income		$118,000

*$600,000 incurred overhead minus $585,000 applied ($315,000 + $270,000)

Problem 2

$$\text{Cost per unit} = \$12.10 = \frac{\$14,410 + \$295,350}{24,000 + (4,000 \times 40\%)}$$

$$\text{Ending inventory} = \$19,360 = 4,000 \times 40\% \times \$12.10$$

Problem 3

Jackson Company
Income Statement for July 19X5

Sales			$262,500
Standard cost of sales	(17,500 × $10)		175,000
Standard gross profit			87,500
Variances:*			
Material use		$ 350U	
Direct labor efficiency		600U	
Variable overhead spending		1,800U	
Variable overhead efficiency		800U	
Fixed overhead budget		700F	
Fixed overhead volume		4,000U	6,850
Actual gross profit			80,650
Selling and administrative expenses			32,400
Income			$ 48,250

*Variances:
  Material use   [36,700 - (18,000 × 2)] × $.50 = $350U
  Direct labor efficiency   [9,100 - (18,000 × .5)] × $6 = $600U
  Variable overhead spending $74,600 - (9,100 × $8) = $1,800U
  Variable overhead efficiency   [9,100 - (18,000 × .5)] × $8 = $800U
  Fixed overhead budget $39,300 - $40,000 = $700F
  Fixed overhead volume   (20,000 - 18,000) × $2 = $4,000

COMPREHENSION CHECK

1. True

2. False: A variance should be investigated if the expected cost to investigate is less than the expected cost of not investigating.

3. True

4. False: Safety stock is the amount of inventory that the firm holds as a buffer against the possibility of late delivery or greater than expected use during the lead time.

5. True

6. False: The salary of the purchasing agent is fixed. Only the incremental costs of placing an order are relevant in determining ordering costs.

7. True   8. True

9. False: Because ordering costs increase with the number of orders placed, which is equivalent to increasing as the order size decreases, the EOQ will increase as ordering costs increase.

10. False: The major cost of not having enough inventory is the opportunity cost of lost sales, which is much harder to estimate than the costs of carrying inventory.

11. False: If the demand for a product is limited, the limitation can be included as one of the constraints.

12. False: The critical question is the contribution margin per unit of the scarce resources available. It is possible that the product with the highest contribution margin requires so much time to produce that it will never be included in the optimal solution.

13. True   14. True

15. False: It indicates that any linear combination of the two can be produced with maximums of 300 of X and 150 of Y.

16. False: The manager should look for resources that have high shadow prices, indicating that higher contribution margin would be earned if they were expanded. A shadow price is the amount to be gained by adding capacity.

APPLICATIONS

Problem 1

The variance should be investigated.

Expected cost to investigate

Outcome	Probability	Cost	Expected Cost
Variance is random	.40	$ 100	$ 40
Problem exists, can be corrected	.48*	100	48
Problem exists, cannot be corrected	.12†	1,600	192
Totals	1.00		$280

*60% × 80%
†60% × 20%

Expected cost of not investigating

	Probability	Cost	Expected Cost
Variance is random	.40	$ 0	$ 0
Problem exists	.60	1,500	900
Totals	1.00		$900

Problem 2

A.   The reorder point is 2,100 bolts [(6,000/300) × 8] + 500

B.   ### Costs of ordering policies

Number of orders	4	5	6
Order costs (number of orders × $180)	$720	$900	$1,080
Quantity ordered (6,000/number of orders)	1,500	1,200	1,000
Average inventory (quantity ordered/2)	750	600	500
Carrying costs (average inventory × $1.50)	$1,125	$900	$750
Total costs (order costs + carrying costs)	$1,845	$1,800	$1,830

Problem 3

The optimal number is 600 heads as calculated in the following tables.

Event—Demand	Conditional Values—Incomes Strategies: Purchases			
	500*	600†	700‡	800§
500	$100	$ 70	$ 40	$ 10
600	100	120	90	60
700	100	120	140	110
800	100	120	140	160

*(500 × $.50) - (500 × $.30)
†(demand × $.50) - (600 × $.30); e.g., (500 × $.50) - (600 × $.30) = $70
‡(demand × $.50) - (700 × $.30); e.g., (600 × $.50) - (700 × $.30) = $90
§(demand × $.50) - (800 × $.30); e.g., (600 × $.50) - (800 × $.30) = $60

		Expected Values: Conditional Values × Probabilities			
Demand, Probability		500	600	700	800
500	20%	$ 20	$ 14*	$ 8	$ 2
600	30%	30	36†	27‡	18
700	30%	30	36	42	33
800	20%	20	24	28	32
Expected values		$100	$110	$105	$ 85

*$70 × 20%
†$120 × 30%
‡$90 × 30%

Problem 4

The graph below shows the solutions under both capacities for department I. The contribution margins at each corner are summarized below.

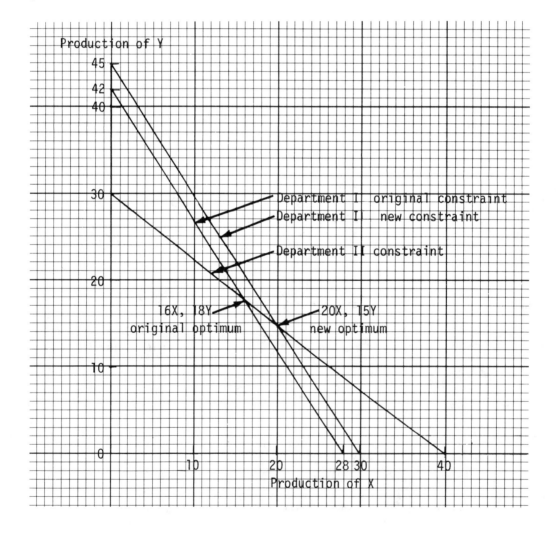

	Original Situation		
Corner	Contribution from X	Contribution from Y	Total Contribution
28X, zero Y	$140	$ 0	$140
zero X, 30Y	0	120	120
16X, 18Y	80	72	152
	Proposed Situation		
30X, zero Y	$150	$ 0	$150
zero X, 30Y	0	120	120
20X, 15Y	100	60	160

The value of the additional capacity is $8, the difference between total contribution margin at the new optimal output and at the original output ($160 - $152).

CHAPTER 16

COMPREHENSION CHECK

| 1. b | 4. a | 6. c | 8. b | 10. b | 12. a | 14. b |
| 2. b | 5. d | 7. a | 9. d | 11. c | 13. d | 15. a |
| 3. a |

APPLICATIONS

Problem 1

Transaction		Cash		Working Capital		Total Assets
0.	+	$10,000	+	$ 4,000	+	$ 4,000
1.		NE		NE	+	$ 8,000
2.	+	$ 5,000		NE		NE
3.	+	$50,000		NE	+	$50,000
4.		NE		NE		NE
5.		NE	-	$ 2,500	-	$ 2,500
6.	-	$ 1,200		NE		NE
7.		NE	-	$ 3,200		NE
8.	+	$ 3,000	+	$ 3,000	+	$ 5,000
9.		NE	-	$ 600	-	$ 600
10.	+	$13,000	+	$13,000	+	$13,000
11.	-	$ 3,000	-	$ 3,000	+	$ 7,000
12.	+	$ 1,800	+	$ 1,800	-	$ 1,000
13.		NE	-	$ 1,000		NE

Problem 2

THRILL COMPANY
Statement of Changes in Financial Position
Cash Basis
for the Year 19X3

Resources provided by:
  Operations:
    Net income $ 3,300
    Adjustments for items that affected
    net income but did not affect cash
    the same way:
      Decrease in accounts receivable $26,700
      Increase in merchandise inventory   (4,100)
      Increase in prepaid expenses   (700)
      Decrease in accounts payable   (15,800)
      Decrease in accrued liabilities   (2,300)
      Increase in income taxes payable   3,800
      Depreciation for the year   17,400
      Gain on sale of land   (3,200)
        Total adjustments   21,800
    Cash provided by operations $25,100
  Cash provided by other sources:
    Proceeds from sale of land   4,900
    Proceeds from issuance of capital stock 28,600
     Total cash provided by other sources   33,500
     Total cash provided during the year   58,600
Resources used for:
  Dividends declared and paid   2,200
  Purchase of new machinery   53,800
    Total cash used during the year   56,000

Increase in cash $ 2,600
Other financing and investing activities:
  Acquisition of machinery through issuance of
  a long-term note payable $18,800

Problem 3

THRILL COMPANY
Statement of Changes in Financial Position
Working Capital Basis
for the Year 19X3

Resources provided by:
  Operations:

Net income			$ 3,300
Adjustments for items that affected net income but did not affect working capital the same way:			
Depreciation for the year		$17,400	
Gain on sale of land		(3,200)	
Total adjustments		14,200	
Working capital provided by operations			$17,500
Other sources:			
Proceeds from sale of land		4,900	
Proceeds from issuance of capital stock		28,600	
Total working capital from other sources			33,500
Total working capital provided during the year			51,000
Resources used for:			
Dividends declared and paid		2,200	
Purchase of new machinery		53,800	
Total working capital used during the year			56,000
Net decrease in working capital			$ 5,000
Other financing and investing activities:			
Acquisition of machinery through issuance of a long-term note payable			$18,800

Proof of net decrease in working capital:

	Effect of Change on Working Capital
Increase in cash	$ 2,600
Decrease in accounts receivable	(26,700)
Increase in inventory	4,100
Increase in prepaid expenses	700
Decrease in accounts payable	15,800
Decrease in accrued liabilities	2,300
Increase in income taxes payable	(3,800)
Net change in working capital, decrease	($ 5,000)

CHAPTER 17

COMPREHENSION CHECK

| 1. d | 3. b | 5. b | 7. b | 9. b | 11. a | 13. c | 15. d |
| 2. c | 4. b | 6. c | 8. a | 10. d | 12. b | 14. c | 16. c |

APPLICATIONS

Problem 1   Calculation of Ratios

a. $3,062/$1,418 = 2.2 to 1

b. ($95 + $224 + $1,090)/$1,418 = 1 to 1

c. $1,090/($7,484/365) = 53.2 days

d. $4,681/[($1,365 + $1,506)/2] = 3.3 times

e. ($385 + $149)/($6,622 + $7,423)/2 = 7.6%

f. $385/[($3,058 + $3,407)/2] = 11.9%

g. $385/65 = $5.92

h. $78/$5.92 = 13.2

i. $2,803/$7,484 = 37.5%

j. $385/$7,484 = 5.1%

k. $4,016/$7,423 = 54.1%

l. $713/$149 = 4.8 times

m. ($385 + $359)/$4,016 = 18.5%

Problem 2   Effects of Transactions on Selected Ratios

1. I	4. N	7. I	10. I
2. D	5. N	8. I	11. N
3. D	6. D	9. N	12. N

Problem 3   Working Backward

a. $15,000. The denominator in both the current and the acid-test ratios.

b. $14,000. This can be computed from the difference between the numerator for the current ratio and the numerator for the acid-test ratio. This amount can be checked by reference to the calculation of average inventory in the denominator of the inventory turnover.

c. $70,000, the difference between sales (numerator of receivables turnovers) and cost of goods sold (numerator of inventory turnovers)

d.   28%, computed as $70,000/$250,000

e. $184,000. Since inventory increased by $4,000 ($14,000 at the end and $10,000 at the beginning), the purchases had to be $4,000 greater than what was sold for the year. (Remember that beginning inventory + purchases - ending inventory = cost of goods sold.)

f.   28.4 days. This can be computed by dividing ending inventory of $14,000 by the average daily cost of sales ($180,000 divided by 365).

g. $12,000. The denominator for "times interest earned" shows that two items are added back to net income of $10,000. (You can verify that $10,000 is the net income by referring to the numerator of the computation of return on sales.) The numerator for "times interest earned" is net income before taxes and interest, and the denominator is the amount of interest. Hence, the $8,000 in the numerator of that computation represents the interest, so the $12,000 must represent the income taxes.

h. $5.00. This can be taken directly from the denominator of the computation of dividend yield.

i. $115,000. Total assets at year-end are $300,000 (see denominator in calculation of return on assets); this must also be the total of liabilities and owners' equity. Equity related to common stockholders is $130,000 (see denominator in calculation of return on common stockholder equity) and preferred stock is given as $55,000, for a total stockholders' equity of $185,000. Hence, total liabilities are $115,000 ($300,000 - $185,000). Although the problem does not specifically state that the second number in any calculation of an average refers to the ending balance (ending receivables, ending inventory, ending assets, etc.), this fact can be readily inferred from the placement of ending inventory in the calculation of inventory turnover.

j. $100,000. If total liabilities are $115,000 (part i) and current liabilities are $15,000 (part a), the long-term liabilities must be the difference.

k.   50%. The firm's earnings per share are $.40 (given as $6,000/15,000), and the dividend per share is $.20 (given as the numerator in the computation of dividend yield.

l.   22.4%. The firm's net income of $10,000 (see part g) plus the depreciation of $28,000 (given in the additional information) would be divided by the total liabilities of $115,000 (from part i) plus preferred stock of $55,000.

m. $4,000. In computing earnings per share of common stock, the numerator is the earnings available to common stockholders, in this case $6,000. All net income is available to common stockholders <u>unless</u> there are preferred dividends. But the net income is $10,000 (see part g). Hence, $4,000 has been subtracted from net income to determine the income available to common stockholders. The $4,000 must be preferred dividends.